Teaching
the
Comparative
Approach
to American
Studies

NEW DIMENSIONS SERIES

Teaching the Comparative Approach to American Studies

by Stanley Seaberg
for the Foreign Policy Association

Manufactured in the United States of America

L. C. Card 78-140593

ISBN 0-690-80689-2

The Foreign Policy Association

The Foreign Policy Association is a private, nonprofit, non-partisan educational organization. Its objective is to stimulate wider interest, greater understanding, and more effective participation by American citizens in world affairs. However, as an organization, it takes no position on issues of United States foreign policy. In its publications the FPA strives to insure factual accuracy, but the opinions expressed are those of the authors and not of the organization.

In preparing this book we are grateful for the advice and assistance of Professors Robin W. Winks of Yale University and E. P. Panagopoulos of San Jose State College; also Henry W. Bragdon of the Phillips Exeter Academy and Douglas McClure of Princeton Day School. For help in suggesting materials, we would like to thank Robert L. Zangrando of the American Historical Association and Professor Paul S. Holbo of the University of Oregon. For editorial direction and supervision of the series, the Foreign Policy Association thanks David C. King, Editorial Director.

JAMES M. BECKER
DIRECTOR
School Services
Foreign Policy Association

CONTENTS

Teaching
the
Comparative
Approach
to American
Studies

Introduction

THE TRADITIONAL SURVEY COURSE IN AMERICAN HISTORY —
with its chronological textbook, its memorization of dates
and events, and its multiple-choice tests—used to seem
a pretty adequate way to teach students about their country's past. Most of us learned our history that way and we
have tended to pass it on to this generation of students
in much the same fashion.

Gradually, though, more and more educators have
come to feel that the old way is no longer satisfactory.
We have slowly become aware that the traditional approaches and methods don't really give the student ade-

quate preparation for living in a global society. Nationalist myths and legends of the uniqueness or superiority of his nation's past and values are unacceptable to today's youth who must cope with the challenges of "planet earth."

In our struggle to make our courses relevant to contemporary life, some important breakthroughs have been made. There is, for example, an increasing awareness that teaching history alone is not enough—that it must be integrated with the discoveries made in other disciplines about our past, our present, and our future. Seemingly diverse fields such as anthropology, economics, and sociology are transforming "history" into "social sciences" and "U.S. History" into "U.S. Studies." In addition, the multiplication of audio-visual materials and experimentation with new ways of learning may help us to emerge from the cramped structures and textbooks of the past.

Despite progress in some areas, the traditional U.S. History course still shows a remarkable resistance to change. The typical course continues to treat our national development as an isolated phenomenon, fostering a narrow, parochial view of our past and our place in the world today. Louis Hartz' observation about American historians applies to high school teachers as well: "the American historian at practically every stage has functioned quite inside the nation; he has tended to be an erudite reflection of the limited social perspective of the average American himself."

Since we can no longer deny the fact that we live in a global community, the teaching of American history must take account of that fact. This does not mean that pride in our nation is dead or that we must foster an idealistic internationalism, but rather that we must teach our students to view their country's history in terms of a world setting and in the light of contemporary concerns.

In other words, what is happening in the world today forces us to change the way we look at our past. This does not imply a distortion of history to fit the images of the present; it means instead that events that were viewed as minor or obscure through a nationalist lens assume new proportions and importance when looked at from an international perspective. British historian Geoffrey Barraclough suggests how present events lead us to take a new look at the past:

> The rising generation will inevitably look back over the twentieth century with different priorities from ours. Born into a world in which—as all present indications suggest—the major questions will not be European questions but the relationships between Europe, including Russia, and America and the peoples of Asia and Africa, they will find little relevance in many of the topics which engrossed the attention of the last generation. The study of contemporary history requires new perspectives and a new scale of values.
>
> Geoffrey Barraclough, *An Introduction to Contemporary History* (Baltimore: Penguin Books, 1967).

Barraclough's point is reinforced by C. Vann Woodward, who notes that "every major historical event has necessitated new views of the past and resulted in reinterpretations of history." The national trauma of Vietnam, for example, has forced national leaders and private citizens alike to a painful re-examination of our values, traditions, and goals. On a less dramatic scale, contemporary experience suggests that topics such as urbanization and the government's role in economic development may become more important study units than the rise of capitalism or the frontier experience. This also means that ideas and ideologies which have previously been taboo, or were treated in Cold War stereotypes of good and bad, will have to be confronted realistically and honestly.

A comparative approach to U.S. studies is no final answer. There is no "new school" of comparative studies, no grandiose scheme to erase the myriad problems faced by the man or woman in the classroom, no easy road to relevancy. Instead, this approach merely suggests ways to enlarge the understanding of our past through comparison and contrast. In one of the major works of scholarship in this area, *The Comparative Approach to American History* (Basic Books, 1968), editor C. Vann Woodward argues that comparative studies: "compel Americans to see their past in a new light; to revise complacent assumptions of national exclusiveness, uniqueness or excellence; to reconsider commonplace myths and flattering legends; and to put to the test of comparison many other traditional assumptions that are rarely subjected to such scrutiny."

Authors of comparative studies are careful to point out that the field of comparative history is new and that the methods are necessarily tentative. In fact, comparisons involving the same events frequently lead to conflicting conclusions; controversy, of course, does not mean the studies are invalid. Students will gain much from the study of conflicting arguments, just as one's views of the American Revolution are sharpened by exploring the opposing theories that the event was either a radical upheaval which gave birth to an age of revolution or an essentially conservative movement designed to maintain the status quo. Keeping these limitations in mind, it is possible to extract, in preliminary form at least, a structure for the comparative method of studying the American experience—a method that offers great promise for updating and internationalizing the teaching of American history.

A word of caution is needed: the comparative approach involves more than a search for easy parallels. There is the danger of over-generalization in simply looking at two events side-by-side. Teachers and students alike should be aware that similarities may be misleading and that contrasts are frequently as instructive as parallels. For example, Seymour Martin Lipset points out in *The First New Nation* (Anchor, 1963) that the problems of nation-building in the early American Republic bore striking resemblances to the problems faced by developing nations today; but to deal only with the similarities could lead to slipshod generalizations. It is equally important to consider the differences, such as the freedom from strong national rivals enjoyed by this country or the fact that the United States developed as a "transplanted" culture.

The high school social studies teacher, then, faces certain difficulties in applying the comparative method to his course. To help avoid the pitfalls of over-generalization and careless parallels, the following five points are offered as guidelines for developing comparative units in U.S. studies:

Political and economic structures of the societies compared should be similar

The development of the United States has been within the framework of the nation-state and within the context of an industrialized economy. Given this setting, it seems likely that the most meaningful comparisons of U.S. experience can be made with the nations of Western Europe and perhaps with non-Western countries like Japan which industrialized at approximately the same time as Western nations. It is perhaps for this reason that the majority of the comparisons in the Woodward volume are with Western countries; the development of European societies parallels that of the United States in industrialization, social democracy, imperialism, urbanization, depression, war, and cold war.

The need for structural similarity, however, does not rule out comparisons with non-Western societies. As C. E. Black has suggested in *The Dynamics of Modernization* (Harper & Row, 1966), the political development of the United States in the early 1800's roughly parallels that of many African and Asian countries today. On the basis of such similarity, Lipset's *The First New Nation* successfully makes use of non-Western sources for comparison with political development in the early American republic.

Experiences or situations compared should be similar, but need not be close in time

In developing comparative units, the teacher will find that many of the events that lend themselves to this approach were shared by other nations at roughly the same time. The American Revolution, of course, was part of a much larger revolutionary movement which swept the entire Western world from the 1760's to the 1850's; the vast migration of European settlers into the open spaces of the Western Hemisphere, Australia, and South Africa suggests comparative studies of frontier movements, slave systems, migration and settlement patterns; the revolutionary process of industrialization absorbed the energies of relatively similar peoples (European) within a relatively similar time span (19th and early 20th centuries) in a series of analagous experiences —economic development, imperialism, urbanization, depression, and wars.

Similarity in time should not be considered an absolute criterion, however. In considering frontier experiences, for example, valid comparisons can be made between the great movements of the nineteenth century and the Russian free frontier movement into Siberia in the early twentieth century, as Donald Treadgold has accomplished in *The Great Siberian Migration* (Princeton, 1957). As has been pointed out, Lipset compares political development in emerging nations today with the American experience in the last century, and Black deals with economic development in much the same manner in *The Dynamics of Modernization* (Harper & Row, 1966).

Validated historical models and hypotheses should be used as guides

Both Lipset and Black make the point that the statistical evidence being used by today's social scientists to make generalizations about urbanization, industrialization, and economic development are partial and incomplete, hence often unreliable. There is a danger, in Lipset's words, that the analyst will unwittingly "find reasons for selecting those indicators which best fit the conceptual framework he is using."

To minimize this danger, Black suggests using institutions for comparison, since they are found in all societies and are readily identifiable. Slavery, as an institution for example, has been successfully studied in comparative perspective by several authors. Other studies have ana-

lyzed military, religious, educational, and business organizations—studies which should be of high interest in
view of the growing concern over "Establishments,"
"Power Structures," and the "Military-Industrial Complex."

Besides the institutional approach, there are a number
of other models that offer possibilities for comparative
studies. The Turner Frontier Thesis, for example, has
been analyzed and criticized at length, and yet is prov-
ing very useful as a model for comparative studies of
Russian, Latin American, Canadian, South African, and
Australian frontier movements. Crane Brinton's thesis on
revolution has been a useful tool for comparison. His
model has been substantially refined and contemporized
by Carl Leiden and Karl M. Schmitt in *The Politics of
Violence: Revolution in the Modern World* (Prentice-
Hall, 1968), a study which combines several theories of
revolution with four case studies—the Turkish, Egyptian, Mexican, and Cuban revolutions.

Comparative method is better suited to the inquiry-inductive approach to learning than to the recitative-expository

The use of models and hypotheses is particularly well
suited to the inquiry approach to learning. Students are
encouraged to develop and test their own theories, to
make inferences and generalizations. Instead of taking
his cues from the teacher or being fed the answers from
a textbook, the student works from a variety of materials
to "inquire" into a particular experience, problem, or
dilemma. Inquiry does not assume final answers but it
does require the student to arrive at generalizations
through a careful process of analysis called the induc-

tive method: forming hypothesis, testing the hypothesis through careful classification and use of evidence, using comparison and contrast, drawing inferences, and making generalizations.

Unfortunately, few of the many projects using the inquiry approach in American studies—the Amherst, Harvard, or Carnegie Tech projects—employ, or even suggest using the comparative approach in a systematic way. The teacher may put together some comparative units by juxtaposing American and non-American sources from the Harvard AEP materials or the Fenton-Carnegie Tech series, but the projects *per se* do not suggest this. An exception may be provided in a recent curriculum study compiled by the California Social Sciences Study Committee. The California report—called the *K-12 Social Sciences Education Framework*—combines the comparative approach with inquiry-conceptual methods throughout the program. The traditional American History course has been expanded into a two-year course in which the American experience is studied in comparison with both Western and non-Western societies.

While it does not use the inquiry approach, *A Free People* (2 vols., Macmillan, 1970) by Bragdon, Cole, and McCutchen, does present the traditional chronology of events within a framework of international and contemporary comparisons. This text, which is also designed for a two-year course, offers a number of stimulating comparative units, with emphasis on Canadian and Mexican events, and generally offers a broader outlook on U.S. history than previous textbooks have done.

The comparative method should seek to develop universal and contemporary generalizations, rather than predetermined generalizations drawn from con-stricted textbooks

If the student uses comparison only to catalogue similarities and differences, very little will be achieved besides rote categorizing. If, however, the student undertakes the study of a vital experience such as revolution, racism or poverty with the purpose of clarifying a pressing social problem in order to achieve more intelligent action, much will have been accomplished.

For example, a comparative study of slavery in the Western Hemisphere should provide considerably more insight into America's present racial problems than would a limited study of slavery in the Ante Bellum South. The student will learn that the difference in legal protections afforded slaves resulted later, after freedom was obtained, in great differences in family life and social organization. Through comparative study, he can better understand the contemporary legacies of slavery in the United States; he begins to see that the problems of black Americans are deeply rooted in historical experience and encompass personal and psychological problems as well as those purely political or economic.

In summary, these criteria suggest that the comparative method involves the use of both similarities and contrasts, with an emphasis on experiences that are shared universally. While it imposes careful limitations to avoid slipshod comparisons, it suggests more exciting methods of investigation and wider possibilities for generalizing about human conduct.

As teachers we tend to worry—perhaps too much—that any new approach to a traditional subject may leave huge gaps in the student's knowledge. The wide acceptance of conceptual frameworks has already shown that such methods actually make retention and understanding easier than the old chronological pegs. The comparative approach offers similar advantages. By giving the student a comparative-international perspective, he is better able to "make sense" out of the crowded events of the past and he begins to get a feel for the ways in which history can help him to understand his world.

In the sections that follow, we will discuss five sample comparative units that the teacher can use as take-off points with a minimum of additional preparation. The materials and approaches suggested are offered as examples only; there is no assumption that they are the best or only way to approach each topic. The final section of the book suggests other areas of study that lend themselves to the comparative approach.

BIBLIOGRAPHY

GENERAL

In recent years, scholars have become increasingly concerned with the reinterpretation of the American past in the light of international and contemporary concerns. One of the major works produced by this scholarship is *The Comparative Approach to American History** (Basic Books, 1968, $2.95), edited by C. Vann Woodward. Using a chronological framework of traditional topics, twenty-two historians attempt to reinterpret the American Revolution, the frontier movement, slavery, Civil War,

---

* Titles marked with an asterisk may be ordered from the World Affairs Book Center, a service of the Foreign Policy Association, 345 E. 46th Street, New York, N.Y. 10017.

industrialization, the Depression, and World Wars within a comparative framework, suggesting new meanings and larger possibilities for the study of the American experience.

While the Woodward volume uses the traditional format of American history courses as the basis for suggesting larger themes, two other books on comparative history offer a somewhat different frame of reference. Seymour Martin Lipset's *The First New Nation** (Anchor, 1963, $1.75) compares the problems of nation-building in the early years of the United States with similar problems faced by the emerging nations of today. *The Dynamics of Modernization** (Harper & Row, $5.95, Torch paperback, $1.60), by C. E. Black, incorporates all contemporary nations within the framework of modern development and suggests major historical patterns for studying contemporary societies. Black discusses the limitations as well as the possibilities of comparative studies and suggests a model for the comparative method.

The Bragdon-Cole-McCutchen text (*A Free People;* vol. 1 *The United States in the Formative Years;* vol. 2 *The United States in the Twentieth Century,* Macmillan, 1970) suggests numerous possibilities for expanding the traditional American history course through comparisons with the experience of other countries.

Geoffrey Barraclough's *Introduction to Contemporary History* (Penguin Books, 1967, $1.25) presents strong arguments for a comparative approach to modern history. Similar explanations of the rationale for this approach are contained in *Generalization in the Writing of History** edited by Louis Gottschalk (University of Chicago Press, 1963, $5.00); and *Theory and Practice in Historical Study* (Bulletin 54, Social Science Research Council, 1946) by John Herman Randall, Jr. and George Haines.

A periodical with a particular interest in the comparative approach is *Comparative Studies in Society and History* (Mouton & Co., Netherlands, 1958—) edited by

Sylvia L. Thrupp. In volume 5 of that journal, an essay by Louis Hartz ("American Historiography and Comparative Analysis") discusses the comparative theme in the writing of U.S. history. Another scholarly journal devoted to comparative analysis is *Comparative Politics* (University of Chicago Press, 1968—).

For discussions of inquiry and inductive methods in the social studies, two very readable books are: Edwin Fenton, *Teaching the New Social Studies in Secondary Schools — An Inductive Approach* (Holt, Rinehart & Winston, 1966, $9.50); and Byron G. Massialas and C. Benjamin Cox, *Inquiry in the Social Studies* (McGraw-Hill, 1966, $7.50).

CURRICULUM PROJECTS

As stated in the introduction, the proposed California *Framework* (State Department of Education, Sacramento, Calif.) offers suggestions for the practical application of the comparative approach. Chapter 3 of this volume, on nationalism, illustrates some of the concepts developed in the *Framework*.

The Committee on the Study of History (The Amherst Project; Director, Dr. Richard H. Brown, The Newberry Library, 60 W. Walton Street, Chicago, Illinois, 60610) has developed curriculum material concerned with discovery learning; one set of units is available through D. C. Heath, and a second group is being published by Addison-Wesley. A listing of other current social studies curriculum projects is available from the Marin Social Studies Project (Director, G. Sidney Lester, Marin County Superintendent of Schools Office, 201 Tamal Vista Blvd., Corte Madera, Calif. 94925) for $3.00.

Studies and materials concerned with comparative analysis of particular subjects will be found in the bibliographies at the close of each of the chapters that follow.

1

The American
Revolution

One of the few topics in the traditional U.S. history course that has long been the basis for comparative analysis has been the American Revolution. Although the subject might not be presented as a comparative study, few teachers would fail to point out some of the relationships between the American and French Revolutions, or the connections between the American experience and the "age of revolution" in general, which swept the Atlantic world between the late 1700's and the mid-nineteenth century. The outlines of a sample unit are presented here partly as a means of creating a transition from familiar areas of comparison to less familiar ones; the purpose is also to suggest some ways in which such a study can be related to topics of current concern, such as violence and protest, and nationalist movements for independence from colonial rule.

Certain difficulties are involved in a comparative approach to the topic of revolution. Scholars, for example, have long argued about what, exactly, constitutes a revolution, and how such an event differs from rebellion, insurrection, or violence as a means of protest. Crane Brinton's *The Anatomy of Revolution* (Random House, Inc., 1957) offers a time-honored model for identifying true revolutions and Carl G. Gustafson's *Preface to History* (McGraw-Hill, 1955) presents this simple definition: revolution is an "overthrow of government by force" in which "a social or economic group is superseded in control of the state by another group under circumstances of violence." But a reading of Franz Fanon's *The Wretched of the Earth* (Evergreen, 1966) or Eldridge Cleaver's *Soul on Ice* (Dell, 1968) gives one a considerably different slant on what revolution is. Or, one might consider the subject in terms of the conclusion drawn by Manfred Halpern ("A Redefinition of the Revolutionary Situation," *Journal of International Affairs*, Vol. XXIII, No. 1, 1969) that the world today is witnessing "history's first common, world-wide revolution." An interesting and rewarding unit could be constructed around deciding just what constitutes a revolution.

Even without going into the matter of definition as a topic, the class should be aware of the question and should avoid using such terms as *revolution, rebellion,* and *violent protest* interchangeably. For example, we all sense certain parallels between the current struggle of American Negroes for equal rights and some of the factors that led to the American Revolution. Yet to conclude from these similarities that the two experiences fall into the same category might be grossly inaccurate. As was stated in the introduction, it is just as important for students to study contrasts between events as to study parallels.

On the subject of these difficulties, the teacher might find it helpful to read R. R. Palmer's essay in Vann Woodward's *The Comparative Approach to American History*, which discusses various theories about the nature of the American Revolution as well as its relation to the "Negro revolution," violence today, and modern movements for national independence. Palmer, for example, warns of the complications involved in drawing comparisons between the American experience and recent nationalist movements in Asia and Africa: "The situation becomes confused when movements of national independence take on a strong social character, and are directed against foreign capitalism, foreign economic control, or foreign ideas, influences, or privileges, as in the Mexican Revolution after 1910, the Cuban Revolution since 1959, and indeed in the Russian and Chinese revolutions also."

The problems of definition will not be so noticeable, of course, in comparing the American Revolution with, say, the French or even the Russian, but caution will be needed in trying to make the study illuminate contemporary events.

Developing Hypotheses

To introduce the topic and to show its relevancy to today's world, the teacher might begin by assigning an initial reading on the causes of the American Revolution, and then ask the students the following questions, which can be kept in mind throughout the study:

1. What are the reasons for unrest and violent protest in this country today?
2. What similarities exist between these reasons and the causes of the American Revolution? What are some of the differences?
3. What factors turned colonial protest into open rebellion?

On the basis of this introductory discussion, students are ready to form hypotheses on the causes of revolution. This might be a good time for the teacher to mention that, although they will frequently be looking at parallels between actual revolutions and contemporary tensions, this does not imply that we are today in the midst of, or on the verge of, events of equal nature. If the inquiry method is new to the class, advise them also that the models they develop are for purposes of examination only—they are not meant to be final answers. In fact, during the course of the study, each student's hypothesis should be changed and modified as he encounters more information.

The same technique of hypothesis formation and testing can be used for studying other aspects of revolution. A second hypothesis model might deal with the question of what happens to people and institutions during a revolution. A third would be concerned with what changes to societies and institutions result from revolutions. And, if time allows, a fourth could center around the question of finding parallels between the American Revolution and contemporary anti-colonial revolutions, or changes and accommodations made in time to defuse protest and avoid revolution.

Two Case Studies in Revolution

Although any number of revolutions might be used for comparison, the two suggested here serve several basic purposes. The French Revolution is probably the experience most obviously comparable to our own, and helps to illustrate the wider impact of the American Revolution on the "age of revolution" in general. A study of the Russian Revolution will enable the students to see ways in which twentieth century revolutions differ from, as well as parallel, earlier revolutions, and will give them some idea of the Russian experience as a model for, and contrast with, third world revolutions.

The American and French Revolutions

A chief difficulty in undertaking a comparative study of the eighteenth century revolutions is that high school texts in American history barely mention the French Revolution, let alone analyze it in depth. A major exception is provided by the Bragdon-Cole-McCutchen text (*A Free People*, 2 vols., Macmillan, 1970), which devotes 10 pages to the French Revolution and points out parallels and contrasts between the two events. If this text is not available, the teacher can borrow a set of world history texts (provided the school is sufficiently flexible in its textbook policy and has enough books available) and have students read an account of the French Revolution. The Stavrianos text, *A Global History of Man* (Allyn & Bacon, 1966) contains a limited but cosmopolitan description of revolutionary nationalism, incorporating the American and French with several other revolutions of the period.

For advanced students or for those wishing to investigate the subject in more depth, the instructor might wish to suggest some of the important works published in paperback (see Bibliography p. 37). For the general student, however, brief descriptive or analytical readings would be preferable. Leo Gershoy's book, *The Era of the French Revolution 1789–1799* (Anvil, 1957), provides eighty pages of first-hand readings drawn from official documents, newspapers, letters, and diaries. Students can make valuable comparisons of official documents (e.g., *The Declaration of Independence* and *Declaration of the Rights of Man*), personalities, causes of the conflicts, and forces at work in the two upheavals. Gershoy's book, for example, contains several readings gauging the American response to the French Revolution (see pages 141–145 and 172–175).

Richard B. Morris' *The American Revolution* (Anvil, 1955)—a collection of documents and first-hand accounts—makes an excellent companion to the Gershoy volume. Students can compare the two to test and validate their own theories of revolution. Morris unfortunately does not carry his study through the Federalist reaction, but he does suggest the important implications which the American Revolution held for the future.

The study of the revolutions should incorporate a variety of activities—investigations of first-hand sources, discussion sessions, role-playing, dramatization, and films. For example, the two revolutions might be compared by having students assume the roles of individuals who participated in or were connected with both events. Lafayette, Franklin, Paine, Citizen Genet, and participants in the XYZ Affair could be used for this purpose. Interesting discussions could be developed by dramatizing events connected with the Alien and Sedition Acts, or by simulated arguments between Federalists and Anti-Federalists concerning the French Revolution. A *Free People* suggests the following comparison:

> Compare the Philadelphia Convention to the French Constituent Assembly. Consider the men who deliberated, the conflicting purposes of the delegates, the crises that invested the meetings with a sense of urgency, and the final results.
>
> Bragdon, Cole, McCutchen, A *Free People* (New York: Macmillan, 1969).

A final evaluation might employ a two or three page essay in which the student demonstrates how his hypotheses were developed, modified, and verified through comparison and how and why he arrived at certain tentative conclusions. In this exercise, the student might use the two brief, contrasting essays by Gentz and Palmer in Edwin Fenton's *32 Problems in World History* (Scott, Foresman, 1969). Students could then re-evaluate their conclusions by reading their essays to each other, discussing points of difference, and debating conflicting interpretations.

The American and Russian Revolutions

Although none of the recent social studies projects explicitly provides an international comparative framework for the American history program, the new methods and materials make it possible for the teacher to develop his own program in comparative history. Two booklets from the Harvard Public Issues Series (American Education Publications), *The American Revolution* and *20th Century Russia,* make an excellent combination for a comparative study of violence and revolution. Both studies require students continuously to compare past and present. The final exercise in *20th Century Russia* offers explicit suggestions for comparing the American and Russian Revolutions.

In the following pages various study exercises from the two booklets will be juxtaposed in order to specify examples and suggest comparisons. During the actual study it is assumed that most classes will first study the American Revolution and then use the Russian experience for purposes of comparison.

First, note the questions that are raised at the beginning of each study:

The American Revolution

What is a proper government, and where does its power originate?

In what ways should people—as groups or individuals—be able to express themselves to constituted authority? And what responsibility do rulers have to listen?

When and how is authority to be challenged? Are there rules which tell us the exact point at which control becomes tyranny? Is there a precise measurement for the point at which dissent may turn to revolt? Is violence ever the "right" course?

The American Revolution (Columbus, Ohio: American Education Publications, 1967).

20th Century Russia

Should change be allowed to arise only "naturally" within a community, or is outside agitation justified in some circumstances?

Is it morally right to use violence to gain political power, and if so, under what circumstances?

To what extent should government be responsible for people deprived of property or security during periods of rapid political and economic change?

To what extent should different levels of government take leadership in promoting drastic changes that will affect large numbers of citizens?

What should be the role and the obligations of an individual caught in the midst of revolutionary mass movements?

Twentieth Century Russia (Columbus, Ohio: American Education Publications, 1968).

Both studies, it is clear, deal with violence, the role of the individual in society, the role of government, and dissent against authority. *The American Revolution* centers more on conflicting values as related to the lives of protagonists in the revolutionary struggle. *20th Century Russia* extends the study of revolution over a much longer time span.

The following exercise from *The American Revolution* illustrates how the student is forced to assess his own values while analyzing those of participants in the revolutionary struggle. In the reading preceding the exercise, a moderate, George Watkins, has been forced to analyze his own values and commitments in discussions with a loyalist conservative, Dr. Soame Johnson, and the colonial rebel, Sam Adams.

Who Should Govern

George Watkins, central figure of the case you have just read, is caught in a conflict of values about government. What is a value? It is a firmly held idea of what is "good" or "right." People often hold strong values to the point that they feel no desire or need to prove them:

"It is good to help other people."

"Why?"

"I don't know, it's just good."

When a person values something for himself—where he has a personal preference—he isn't usually pressed very hard to defend it. He simply prefers onions or carrots, or pistachio or chocolate ice cream; no one will argue seriously against such likes or dislikes. A person's values for the society or the community, however, may be a different matter than personal preferences.

Many different values can be expressed about government. The person expressing values about government—what is good for himself and others—will usually find himself obliged to justify them if he can.

Check Your Values. On the next page are ten value statements about government. Put a checkmark ($\sqrt{}$) in the column to the left of those statements which represent the values you hold about "good" government. Compare the set of values you have checked with those checked by your fellow students. Are your values alike or different?

Classify Values. Each of the statements can be identified and classified as a different value. In column A on the next page, mark each statement with the letter of the one classification which you think fits it best:

(A) Competence and "know-how"
(B) Tradition or familiar customs
(C) Religion, belief in a Supreme Being
(D) Law, the written and spoken rules of the society
(E) Separated power

(F) Strength—"might makes right"
(G) Property ownership
(H) Impartiality
(I) Majority rule
(J) Efficiency

Recognizing Values of Others. In the previous case study George Watkins, Dr. Soame Johnson, and Samuel Adams seem to hold different values. Review the case. Then, in column B on the next page, mark the initials of each man next to all the value statements you think he supports. Which two of the three men have the strongest differences between them? You may observe that Watkins is in a dilemma, that he himself holds values that conflict with one another.

Are there values expressed in *The Case of George Watkins* which are not represented in the list on the next page? Identify any others you can find in the case.

A B

1. It would be wrong to change the system of government we have inherited. It has the benefits of long experience.		
2. A leader is not finally responsible to the people, but only to God, from whom he receives authority.		
3. Fair decisions can be made only by impartial leaders who have no special interest whatsoever at stake. Only these people should be allowed to govern.		
4. Leaders should not bow to the prejudiced interest of the people, but should be guided by a sense of law. Legal rights and the general welfare should be their only guidelines.		
5. Each man should have a say in determining his own fate. Thus, the government should be run by representatives chosen by a majority of the people.		

	A	B
6. A country belongs to those men who own property in it, and they should govern.		
7. Power should be separated and divided among several ruling groups. Centralized power often brings tragic mistakes.		
8. The power to govern should be given to the most capable people, to those who have demonstrated intelligence and skill. The average man does not have enough skill to govern his fellowmen.		
9. Life is naturally a struggle. Those strong enough to seize power can earn the right to govern.		
10. Time, money, and effort are saved when a small, unified group runs the government. It is inefficient and wasteful to split power among groups who will bicker and delay decisions.		

The American Revolution (Columbus, Ohio: American Education Publications, 1967).

The Russian study does not include a conflicting-values chart, but the readings incorporate values held by workers, students, soldiers, peasants, and Czar. The class could use the same chart or, as an inquiry exercise, develop a modified version for analyzing conflicting values in the Russian Revolution.

Both studies attempt to get students to consider the use of violence as a means of protest, and both continuously draw connections between past and present. For example, the unit on the American Revolution uses the following exercises to get students involved in the controversies of protest and change. The first set follows a section of readings describing the Stamp Act protest.

1. Defining Patriotism. John Adams, as you know, was to become a great American leader and second President of the U.S. But what about his attitudes and his loyalties in the Stamp Act crisis? Do you think it would be fair or unfair to call his reactions unpatriotic? Why? Do you think it would be fair or unfair to say that he was more interested in his personal welfare than in the good government of England or the American colonies? Why?

2. Defining Legality. Patrick Henry was widely regarded as a radical. His seven resolutions helped crack strong bonds between England and the colonies. Yet they were presented and put to vote in an established legislature. Under these circumstances, would you say that Patrick Henry was basically a lawmaker or lawbreaker? Why?

3. Judging Methods of Protest. The American colonies' uproarious response to the Stamp Act involved many methods of protest. Among them were:

a. hanging effigies
b. destroying private property
c. parading in orderly demonstrations
d. petitioning the government
e. writing sets of resolutions
f. boycotting products
g. intimidating government officials
h. writing articles against the government
i. physically attacking government officials

Choose five of these methods and indicate how they appeared in the Stamp Act protest. Then indicate those which you think were effective in accomplishing what they were intended to do. Finally, indicate those which you think most easy to justify as "right" under the circumstances of 1765.

The second follows a description of the Pettus Bridge confrontation during the Selma civil rights march.

Analyzing Parallels. The questions of authority and dissent in Selma, Alabama, in 1965 and in the American colonies in 1765–1773 invite the making of comparisons and contrasts. Consider these questions in terms of the Selma case and of the Stamp Act case, pages 14–24:

1. Suppose that a speaker said that the Rev. Martin Luther King was the "Sam Adams of our time." On what specific grounds would you agree or disagree with this comparison?

2. Who, in your opinion, had the more serious grievances, the Stamp Act opponents of 1765 or the opponents of Selma's voter registration practices in 1965? Give specific reasons for your opinion.

3. Did the Stamp Act opponents have greater opportunity or less opportunity than the Selma demonstrators to have complaints heard by established authorities? Give specific reasons for your opinion.

4. Did either the Stamp Act or the Selma voter registration practices involve issues that would remain even if these particular conflicts had been peacefully resolved? Give specific reasons for your opinion.

5. Compare or contrast the methods of protest employed against the Stamp Act in the colonies and against voter registration practices in Selma. Were the 1765 methods of protest more effective or less effective than the 1965 methods of protest? Were the 1765 methods of protest more easily justifiable or less easily justifiable as "right" than the 1965 methods of protest? Give specific reasons for your opinion.

6. Which established authorities, those of the colonies in 1765 or of Selma in 1965, acted more closely in accordance with the laws of their own place and time? Do you think that constituted authorities in either case could have finally adopted policies which could be more easily justified as "right"? Give specific grounds for your opinions.

7. Did the Stamp Act protest or the Selma protest have more popular support? Should the "rightness" of

either one be measured in terms of public support?
Give specific grounds for your opinions.

The American Revolution (Columbus, Ohio: American
Education Publications, 1967).

20th Century Russia uses the comparison of present
and past much more extensively than *The American
Revolution*—to the extent of probably forcing some of
the comparisons. In the following exercise, the authors
challenge students to consider violent protest as a means
of political change following a series of personal accounts
of protest during the 1905 revolution in Russia.

1. Marxist Theory and Revolutionary Russia. According to the theories of Karl Marx, conflict between
social classes is inevitable in every society. That is, the
lower classes (the oppressed) will successfully rebel
against the upper classes (the oppressors) in a class
struggle. In modern times, *feudalism* (rule by the no-
bility) has given way to *capitalism* (rule by busi-
nessmen). (Lenin asserted that a stage of autocracy or
dictatorship came before capitalism.) Capitalism is
doomed to yield in turn to rule by the proletariat, or
working class. With the proletariat in control, the means
of production will then be held by the state in a *so-
cialistic* system. Ultimately, Marx predicted, society
will stabilize with communism—a stage in which the
state has "withered away."

To what extent does Marxist theory accurately apply
to conditions in the Russia of 1905? To what extent
does it apply to the United States? Have there been
class struggles in the United States and are there any
today?

2. Students in Revolt. In April of 1968 about 200
students at Columbia University seized five major
buildings. They held one dean prisoner for more than
24 hours, and ransacked the president's office. The
rebels said that they were protesting the planned con-

Anti-Vietnam war protest in New York's Central Park

Photo: Bernard P. Wolff

struction of a university gymnasium in Morningside Park, a project they felt would deprive Harlem residents of an important recreation area. Another complaint of the rebels was Columbia's cooperation with the Institute of Defense Analysis on military projects. A third motive was to win an amnesty for students demonstrating on the first two issues.

At first the Columbia administration attempted to take the disorder in stride. Negotiations were offered. But rebel leaders were not easily reconciled.

Finally, after a week of the occupation, the Columbia administration called in the police. Police officers forcefully cleared out the buildings and arrested 720 students. Charges of brutality generated sympathy for the striking students among both neutral students and faculty members.

Some of those joining in the seizure of Columbia buildings were black militants concerned with racial issues. But the more numerous white rebels tended to have sweeping objectives, including major changes in American political and economic institutions. According to a *New York Times* report, these white activists typically came from prosperous families living on the eastern seaboard. Contrary to common belief, most parents of the activists seemed to back or sympathize with the militancy of their children.

Despite the success of the rebels in disrupting Columbia, a poll conducted by Columbia's Bureau of Applied Social Research indicated that only a minority of the student body sympathized with the *tactics* of the rebellion. According to the poll, 68 percent of Columbia students and 77 percent of the faculty disapproved of the tactics. Nevertheless, a slight majority of those polled supported the stated *objectives* of the rebels.

In what ways were the student revolts of 1905 in Russia and the rebellion of 1968 at Columbia similar and different? Consider such aspects as the following:

a. social class of students
b. long-range objectives of students

    c. response of university authorities
    d. response of government and law officers
    e. alternative ways of protesting

Given the circumstances of both groups of students, which group was more justified in taking the action it did? Why?

Twentieth Century Russia (Columbus, Ohio: American Education Publications, 1967).

Following a study of the Stalin era, the final section of *20th Century Russia* encourages students to attempt a more comprehensive comparison of American and Russian revolutions. Students are challenged to consider the long-range consequences of revolutions as well as their causes and more immediate effects. This challenging exercise requires more information than the booklet offers, which might make it a useful opportunity for independent study and investigation.

Kinds of Revolution: In how many ways were the American Revolution and the Russian Revolution truly revolutionary? In what ways did they change such things as these:

a. The opportunity for any person to rise to a higher position of public respect or economic well-being
b. The operation of government and the opportunity for people to participate in government
c. The opportunity for people to make decisions about such things as the kind of work they wish to do, where they wish to live, and how they wish to think and express themselves
d. The opportunity for people to be protected from being controlled directly or indirectly by their government?

e. Are either of these two revolutions over? The American Declaration of Independence says that ". . . *Governments are instituted among men, deriving their just powers from the consent of the governed . . . Whenever any form of government becomes destructive of these ends, it is the right of the people to alter or to abolish it, and to institute new government.*"

Later Thomas Jefferson wrote that "The tree of liberty must be refreshed from time to time with the blood of patriots and tyrants."

Did the statement from the Declaration of Independence apply only to the time in which it was written? Or has the American Revolution continued, as Thomas Jefferson suggested it should? In what ways, if any, would you say that it continues?

Do further research in history and current affairs, and consider whether or not the Russian Revolution has been completed.

The Consequences of Revolutions: In June 1968 a Russian physicist, Andrei D. Sakharov, published an unusual essay. He suggested that the United States and the Soviet Union were already very much alike, and should be working to bring their political and economic systems still closer together. When this happened, he proposed, the two nations should join hands and work together to solve world problems of peace and economic security.

Other observers have been more and more impressed with the similarity between the United States and the Soviet Union rather than with their differences. It may be that the use of modern technology in the production of economic goods and services, the development of mass culture through modern communications, and the reduction of pressures of security insurance are much more important in determining styles of life than the specific features of a political or economic system— capitalism, socialism, democracy.

To expand discussion of these ideas, try to get information concerning the ways in which the life of the average person in the Soviet Union is similar to and different from the life of the average person in the United States.

Twentieth Century Russia (Columbus, Ohio: American Education Publications, 1967).

Summary

If the study of revolution has been done in sufficient depth, students should have a valuable working hypothesis and tool which can be used for analyzing revolution and violent changes in other eras and societies. This comparative study should help provide the "structure" and "transfer" of knowledge which Jerome Bruner and others suggest as central to the learning process. It should be apparent, for example, that the hypotheses about revolution can be a useful tool in analyzing what many historians refer to as "The Second American Revolution"—The Civil War—as well as numerous twentieth century revolutions—Chinese, Algerian, Cuban and African and Vietnamese.

Obviously, a one-year course cannot possibly encompass all revolutions or else the study of revolutions would consume the entire year. One of the recent or contemporary revolutions, however, might be given special emphasis. At the very least, students will approach the study of contemporary revolutions with a more objective, scientific attitude than the simplistic good and bad analysis of Cold War politics. It may even lead the teacher of American history to question the parochial quality of the course he is teaching and to ask whether he and the fellow next door teaching world history might have something in common.

Checksheet for Analyzing Revolutions

Students and teachers may find the following checksheet useful for analyzing the extent of revolutionary change.

A. Causes	1	2	3
1. Weakening of political authority and instituitions	Partial ☐	Substantial ☐	Complete ☐
2. Criticism of existing system by writers and intellectuals.	Partial and Sporadic ☐	Substantial and relatively sustained ☐	Complete and continuous ☐
3. Violence, riots and assassinations.	Sporadic ☐	Often and increasing ☐	Continuous ☐

B. Revolutionary Changes

1. Transfer of power to revolutionaries	Peaceful ☐	Voluntary after substantial violence ☐	Violent overthrow ☐
2. Civil war	Small segments of population ☐	Substantial. Partial breakdown of economy ☐	Almost total. Economy is disrupted ☐
3. Program of revolutionary change a. Political system and institutions	Partial ☐	Substantial ☐	Almost complete ☐

b. Economic system and institutions ☐ ☐ ☐

c. Social classes and institutions ☐ ☐ ☐

C. The Results of Revolution

	Older groups return to power	Substantial numbers of the older groups return	Few or none of the older groups return
1. Conservative reaction in which many of the older political, economic, and social classes are returned to power.	☐	☐	☐

	Limited	Substantial	Extensive
2. The government becomes more centralized.	☐	☐	☐
3. The economy is industrialized.	☐	☐	☐
4. The political, material, and social conditions of citizens improve.	☐	☐	☐
5. A national cultural awakening occurs.	☐	☐	☐
6. International alliances and trade are extended.	☐	☐	☐
7. Imperialist ventures are undertaken.	☐	☐	☐

Tentative analysis: If ten or more checks occur in categories two and three, a relatively extensive revolution marked by

long range institutional and value changes has probably occurred. If ten or more checks occur in categories one and two,
the revolution was partial or incomplete.

BIBLIOGRAPHY

GENERAL

A detailed comparative analysis of eighteenth century
revolutions is presented in Robert R. Palmer's two volume study, *The Age of the Democratic Revolution**
(Princeton, 1959, 1963, $10.00 each). Palmer places the
American Revolution within the context of the revolutionary movement which affected Atlantic civilization
from 1760 to 1848. *The Age of Revolution** (Mentor,
1962, $1.25) by E. J. Hobsbaum connects and explains
the twin revolutions, political and industrial, which
transformed Europe and the world. A highly interpretive
study, *The Price of Revolution** (Universal Library, 1951,
1966, $2.50) by D. W. Brogan, questions the long-term
effects and ultimate benefits of revolution upon our present troubled age.

A somewhat different approach to revolution is offered
by Barrington Moore, Jr. in *Social Origins of Dictatorship and Democracy** (Beacon Press, 1966, 1967, $2.95).
Moore argues from the perspective of economic change
and views the American Civil War as part of a larger
revolutionary transition from agrarian to industrial societies. *The Politics of Violence: Revolution in the Modern
World** (Prentice-Hall, 1968, $2.45) by Carl Leider and
Karl M. Schmitt is an analysis of contemporary revolu-

* Titles marked with an asterisk may be ordered from the World
Affairs Book Center, a service of the Foreign Policy Association,
345 E. 46th Street, New York, N.Y., 10017.

tionary movements following the Brinton comparative approach. The first half of the book is analytical and historiographical; the second part consists of four concise case studies of revolution—Turkish, Egyptian, Mexican, and Cuban. Volume XXIII, Number 1 of the *Journal of International Affairs* (Columbia University, 1969—) is devoted to the topic: "Political Conflict; Perspectives on Revolution."

THE AMERICAN REVOLUTION

In addition to the materials discussed in the text of this chapter, two readable accounts of the American Revolution, both highly favorable to the American cause and viewing American grievances as real and justifiable, are: *The Birth of the American Republic* (Chicago, 1956, $1.75) by Edmund Morgan and *Origins of the American Revolution** (Stanford, 1959, $3.75) by John C. Miller. A view of revolution more supportive of the British imperial interpretation is argued by Lawrence H. Gipson in *The Coming of the Revolution 1763–1775** (Torchbook, 1962, $1.95). The novels of Esther Forbes (*Johnny Tremain*), Kenneth Roberts (*Oliver Wiswell, Northwest Passage*), and Howard Fast (*April Morning*) provide fictional accounts of the revolutionary era.

THE FRENCH REVOLUTION

The Old Regime and the French Revolution* (Anchor, 1955, $1.45) by Alexis De Tocqueville presents an analysis of the disintegration of the French nobility as a cause of the French Revolution. A compact, readable account tracing the stages and roles of social classes is Georges Lefebvre's *The Coming of the French Revolution** (Vintage, 1947, $1.25). Robert R. Palmer's *Twelve Who Ruled** (Princeton, 1941, $2.45) evaluates the conflicting roles of participants and leaders in the great event. Fictional sources include Charles Dickens' classic *Tale of Two Cities* and Stendhal's portrait of post-revolutionary society in *The Red and the Black*.

THE RUSSIAN REVOLUTION

An exciting and graphic personal portrayal of the Russian Revolution is the eyewitness account of the American journalist John Reed, *Ten Days That Shook the World** (Signet, 1967, $.75). Virtually the same freshness is achieved in a recent volume of readings edited by Robert Pethybridge, *Witnesses to the Russian Revolution** (Citadel, 1964, 1968, $2.45). Bertram D. Wolfe's *Three Who Made a Revolution** (Delta, 1948, 1964, $2.95) is a combination biography of Lenin, Trotsky, and Stalin. A very readable version for high school students is Alan Moorehead's *The Russian Revolution* (Bantam, 1958, $.75).

The rich number of fictional sources include Boris Pasternak's *Doctor Zhivago* (Signet, 1960, $.95); Mikhail Sholokhov's *And Quiet Flows the Don* (Signet, 1934, 1964, $2.45), *The Don Flows Home to the Sea* (Signet, 1940, 1960, $.75); and Boris Pilnyak's *Mother Earth and Other Stories* (Anchor, 1968, $1.45).

OTHER REVOLUTIONS

A great many paperbacks offer firsthand accounts of revolution in various countries. On the Chinese revolution, Jan Myrdal's *Report From a Chinese Village** (Signet, 1965, $.95) and William Hinton's *Fanshen** (Vintage, 1968, $2.95) draw primarily on original Chinese sources. *The Wretched of the Earth** (Evergreen, 1966, $1.95) by Franz Fanon has become a classic theoretical guide for Third World revolutions as well as an account of the Algerian rebellion. Among many sources on the

Cuban Revolution, Che Guevara's *Reminiscences of the Cuban Revolutionary War** (Grove, 1968, $.95) and Jose Yglesias' *In the Fist of Revolution** (Pantheon, 1968, $5.95) provide contemporary and post-revolutionary accounts. Fictional accounts of the Mexican Revolution now published in paperback include Mariano Azuela's *The Underdogs* (Signet, 1962, $.60), and *Two Novels of Mexico* (University of California Press, 1965, $1.25), and *The Eagle and the Serpent* (Dolphin, 1965, $1.45) by Luis Guzman.

FILMS

"Red China," an NBC White Paper available through Contemporary Films, traces the long struggle between Communist and Nationalist forces in China and briefly describes the changes wrought by the Communist triumph. "Castro" (Contemporary), a documentary from the award-winning biography series produced by David Wolper, is an account of Fidel Castro's role in bringing about the Cuban Revolution. And, of course, a great many television documentaries exploring various areas of violent protest and unrest in today's world are now available at modest rentals. Catalogues offering descriptive listings of short films (including television documentaries) can be ordered from Association Films, 600 Madison Avenue, New York, N.Y.; and Contemporary Films (McGraw-Hill), 245 Park Avenue, New York, N.Y. In addition, a number of universities, such as Syracuse, Indiana, and University of California at Berkeley, offer films for rental to schools.

2

Multi-Racial Societies

RECENT YEARS HAVE WITNESSED MUCH NEEDED, ALTHOUGH belated, attempts to define the role of the black in American History. Occasionally this effort appears strained, as textbook writers seek to graft bits and pieces of the black experience onto traditional white history courses.

The comparative approach may suggest a more realistic means of understanding the historical role and current aspirations of black Americans. For example, a comparison of the slave system in the United States with that of Brazil would reveal some striking features—namely, that the American slave did not enjoy the legal institutional protections possessed by his Latin American counterpart. This lack of protection, in turn, helped create the subservient role forced on the freed slave, and, combined with miscegenation between white master and black female, contributed to the breakdown of family ties. Even a superficial comparison should help the student to a better understanding of the problems faced by black Americans.

Developing Hypotheses

The initial class session could profitably begin with a discussion of current racial tensions in the United States, using the following questions to stimulate discussion:

1. What are some of the causes of racial tension?
2. How many of these causes of tension are rooted in past events?
3. How have relations between blacks and whites changed in recent years?
4. How have other societies faced problems of segregation and discrimination?
5. How have other minority groups in this country been discriminated against?
6. In what ways does their experience differ from the black's?

Following the initial discussion, it would be well to explore these questions in a more systematic manner. Readings from current periodicals could be assigned. Films, used to introduce the topic, could provide the background information to help the student form an initial hypothesis. Television documentaries on race problems are readily available at modest rentals. A very good introduction to this unit would be provided by a pair of films available through the NET Film Service: *Slavery,* and *Brazil: The Vanishing Negro* (30 minutes each).

The development of hypotheses might center around questions such as:

1. What historical factors have determined present-day problems and relationships between racial groups?

2. What present-day factors are causing changes in traditional patterns of race relations?

The first question can be used to develop hypotheses for studying the period of slavery and early years of emancipation. By comparing the experience of the American black slaves and slaves of another society—e.g., Brazil or South Africa—the student should gradually come to see the ways in which the experience of the black American is unique and the ways in which it is similar to that of minority groups in other societies. As he gains in understanding, his hypotheses will be modified and refined until they become useful tools that can be applied to other areas.

Similarly, the second can give rise to hypotheses which would be used for studying current trends in the United States and comparing or contrasting them with other multiracial societies.

The Historical Experience

A number of recent publications on race relations are designed for high school use. One of the most useful for a comparative study is Richard B. Ford's *Tradition and*

Change in Four Societies (Holt Social Studies Curriculum, Edwin Fenton, editor). Ford presents excellent reading materials, graphs, and inquiry exercises on both Brazil and South Africa. Each study is divided into a section on historical development and a section on contemporary race relations.

Although the Ford volume does not include a case study of race relations in the United States to use comparatively with the studies of Brazil and South Africa, a number of inexpensive booklets are available for high school use. A good companion study for the Ford book is Stanley Seaberg's *The Negro in American History;* vol. 1, *Which Way to Citizenship* (Scholastic Book Services, 1969). The Seaberg booklet, which covers the periods of slavery and Reconstruction, leans heavily on firsthand accounts, which fit in well with the readings supplied by Ford.

Parts I–III (pp. 9–66) of the Seaberg booklet offer a selection of accounts by slaves, free Negroes, observers, and historians on the condition of slavery and on relations between blacks and whites. Factors such as frontier conditions, cultural differences, racial antagonism, caste status, and economic needs can be drawn from the readings in the Ford book; comparative readings would come from the sections titled "The Development of Society in the Republic of South Africa" and "The Beginnings of Interracial Contact in Brazil."

The following questions might be used as discussion guides to help students focus more clearly on the issues:

1. How did legal protections granted to slaves in each of the three societies differ? How might these differences affect the black's place in society after emancipation?

2. Following emancipation in the U.S., the black was faced with the so-called "Black Codes." What were these codes? Why were they used? What effect did they have on relations between the races? Were similar laws used to limit the rights of freedmen in either of the other two societies?

3. In Brazil, emancipation (1888) was greeted with a five-day national holiday. What factors contributed to this contrast with our own experience?

4. Some American blacks have said that they would rather live in South Africa than in the United States because then they would at least "know where they stood." What does this statement reveal about the differences in race relations?

5. In which of the three societies did religion have the most important influence on the institution of slavery? Explain.

6. What distinctions were made between a slave and a free white man in each of the societies? What significance might these differences have after emancipation?

7. How much of their tribal culture was retained by the slaves in each of the three systems? Account for the differences.

Study Units

The two sets of essays introduced below are intended to illustrate how the questions raised at the beginning of this chapter can be used to organize study materials. Each organizing question is followed by an introduction and suggested approaches for analysis.

What historical factors have determined present-day problems and relationships between racial groups?

In this exercise, the students should read two essays from Ford's *Tradition and Change in Four Societies;* the first, by Frank Tannenbaum, compares slave systems in Brazil and the United States; the second, by Charles Wagley, compares the same two societies from the perspective of contemporary race relations.

As they read Tannenbaum's essay ("Church, State, and Slavery") have the students list contrasts and parallels between slave societies in Brazil and the United States. The questions with which Ford introduces the essay will help them to focus on some of the major contrasts:

> 1) What is the author's hypothesis about the influence of the Church and the Brazilian government on the institution of slavery?
> 2) What laws did the Brazilian government pass to regulate slavery? What was the tradition upon which these laws were based? Did these laws give any advantages to the Brazilian slave?
> 3) What were the differences in the process of emancipation in the United States and Brazil?
> 4) Did the influence of Church and State bring about accommodation or assimilation of the races in Brazil?
>
> Richard B. Ford, *Tradition and Change in Four Societies* (New York: Holt, Rinehart & Winston, 1968).

The following excerpt from the essay illustrates some of the contrasts the students will encounter:

> . . . Nothing said above must induce the reader to believe that slavery was anything but cruel. It was often

brutal. The difference between the systems lies in the fact that in the Spanish and Portuguese colonies the cruelties and brutalities were against the law, that they were punishable, and that they were perhaps not so frequent as in the British West Indies and the North American colonies. But these abuses had a remedy at law, and the Negro had a means of escape legally, by compulsory sale if the price were offered, and by many other means. More important was the fact that the road was open to freedom, and once free, the Negro enjoyed, on the whole, a legal status equal to that of any other subject of the king or to that of any other citizen of the state. And if the question of color was an issue, he could purchase "whiteness" for a specific price . . .

The different ways in which slavery was finally abolished in the two areas (Latin America and the United States) illumine the social process of which they were an integral part. In the Latin-American area slavery and freedom were, socially and morally speaking, very close to each other. The passage from slavery to freedom was always possible for the individual, and in practice frequent. There was nothing final or inescapable in the slave status. In fact, the contrary was the case. The social structure was malleable (flexible), the gap between slavery and freedom narrow and bridgeable, and almost any slave could hope that either he or his family would pass over from his side of the dividing line to the other. Easy manumission all through the period meant that there were always a large number of people in the community who had formerly been slaves and were now free. This is one of the two crucial differences between the character and the outcome of the slave institution in the Latin-American scene on the one hand and in the United States on the other. The second basic difference was to be found in the position of the freedman after manumission. In fact, in Latin America there was for legal and practical purposes no separate class of freedmen. The freedman was a free man. In the Latin-American slave system the easy and continuous change of status implied a process of evolution and a capacity for absorption within the social structure that prevented the society from hardening and kept it from becoming divided. . . . There is, in fact, from this point of view, no slave system; there are only individual slaves. There is no slave by nature, no absolute identification of a given group of individuals as slaves, to whom and to whose children the hope of escape from the hardships they are suffering is forever denied.

If in Latin America the abolition of slavery was achieved . . . without violence, without bloodshed, and without civil war, it is due to the fact that there was no such fixed horizontal division, no such hardening of form that the pattern could no longer change by internal adaptations. In the Latin American area the principle of growth and change had always been maintained. In the United States the very opposite had come to pass. For reasons of historical accident and conditioning, the Negro became identified with the slave, and the slave with the eternal pariah (outcast) for whom there could be no escape. The slave could not ordinarily become a free man, and if chance and good fortune conspired to endow him with freedom, he still remained a Negro, and as a Negro, according to the prevailing belief, he carried all of the imputation of the slave inside him. In fact, the Negro was considered a slave by nature, and he could not escape his natural shortcomings even if he managed to evade their legal consequences. Freedom was made difficult of achievement and considered undesirable both for the Negro and for the white man's community in which the Negro resided. The distinction had been drawn in absolute terms, not merely between the slave and the free man, but between the Negro and the white man. The contrast was between color—the Negro was the slave, and the white man was the free man. Attributes (characteristics) of a sharply different moral character were soon attached to these different elements in the population, and they became incompatible with each other. They might as well, so far as the theory was concerned, have been of different species, for all of the things denied to the Negro as a slave were permitted to the white man—as a citizen. . . .

Richard B. Ford, *Tradition and Change in Four Societies* (New York: Holt, Rinehart & Winston, 1968).

On the basis of their analyses of differences and similarities under slavery, ask the students what they would expect black-white relationships to be like under a free system in an urban society. They should consider social class, employment, attitudes, values and customs.

Before going on to the Wagley essay, have students compare their projections and critically evaluate each other's suggestions. Students can then check their predictions against Wagley's essay. A follow-up discussion can determine why students develop particular projections and why the societies developed differently from some of the students' suppositions.

As the following excerpts from Wagley's essay ("Race and Class in Brazil: A Summary") suggest, sorting out the precise relations between races in Brazil will not be an easy task:

It is one of the most cherished national themes that Brazil is a racial democracy. Since the abolition of slavery in 1888, there has been no legal form of racial discrimination or segregation in Brazil. Innumerable individuals of Negroid or mixed physical appearance have filled important roles in Brazil's national life since the time of the empire. All books on Brazil cite names of Negroes and mulattoes of importance . . .

The world championship soccer team of 1962 covered the whole spectrum of skin color: Pele, the "King of Soccer," who is a Negro, was injured but was competently replaced by Amarildo, a mulatto. Several

players were clearly white. This tradition of racial democracy is a source of pride to Brazilians. More than
any other country in the Western world, Brazil is
recognized, cited, and applauded as proof that racial
democracy can work. But the facts of Brazilian race and
class relations are not as simple as that. They require
some explanation, sometimes even to Brazilians themselves. . . .

Perhaps the most important difference between
race relations in Brazil and in the United States is that
color is but one of the criteria by which people are
placed in the total social hierarchy. Before two Brazilians decide how they ought to behave toward each
other, they must know more than the fact that one is
dark-skinned and the other light-skinned. A Brazilian is
never merely a white man or a man of color; he is a
rich, well-educated white man of a good family or a
poor, uneducated white man from the *povo;* he is a
well-educated mulatto with a good job, or a poor, uneducated Negro. Other criteria, such as income, education, family connections, and even personal charm
and special abilities or aptitudes come into play when
placing a person in terms of the prestige hierarchy or
even of social class. Above all, these multiple criteria
determine who will be admitted to hotels, restaurants,
and most social clubs; who will get preferential treatment in stores, churches, nightclubs, and travel convey-
ances (vehicles); and who will have the best chance
among a number of marriage suitors.

The existence of recognized intermediate types is
important to the understanding of the Brazilian race-
class system and to its functioning. To put it simply, a
two-fold Jim Crow system could never work in Brazil.
A mulatto is not a Negro, and a *moreno* (dark-white)
is not a mulatto. If Brazilians wanted to install a Jim
Crow system, they would have to provide at least four
or more sets of schools, hospitals, sections on public
transportation, and restaurants . . .

Richard B. Ford, *Tradition and Change in Four Societies*
(New York: Holt, Rinehart & Winston, 1968).

What present-day developments are causing changes in traditional patterns of race relations?

For this phase of the unit, the class will be reading descriptions of transition in three multi-racial states: the United States, Brazil, and Rhodesia. Again, as they read, ask them to note down similarities and differences. Their lists of similarities are likely to include migration, urbanization, family disintegration, rebellious ness of youth, racial prejudice, and activities controlled by city officials and bureaucracies. Differences will probably center around environment and degrees of poverty.

The students will be quick to recognize that urbanization is affecting people everywhere in similar ways. Movement to the city breaks up traditional family social patterns, creating rebellious youth and numerous social problems that seem to accompany urban life. Another factor of importance is the continuous contact with government through police, welfare officials, and agencies of national government. Even though minorities may feel mistreated or abused, their lives are closely connected with—and often dependent upon—the myriad arms of government.

Following are excerpts from readings describing part of the racial predicament faced by each of the three societies:

> Then, in the mid-1950's, the operation of the coal mine in Hanna, like that of many small mines from Kentucky to Washington, had begun to peter out. Wallace Frye, an Oklahoma cotton farmer who had been recruited by the United Mine Workers in 1944 when there had been a shortage of miners, had to start thinking about moving. Nor was it only a question of moving.

Wallace Frye had two skills: cotton farming and coal mining. Technological changes had made a manpower surplus in both. Now, in middle age, he was cast out to become part of that vast minority army, jobless and with no real prospect of ever again being able to gain anything but marginal employment. Having relatives in Los Angeles, he decided to transport his second wife, Rene, his stepson Marquette, and the other children to Southern California.

The Fryes arrived in Los Angeles in 1957. From a truly integrated community they were plunged into the heart of a ghetto, where a white face was seen more rarely than in Negro sections of the Black Belt. Wallace Frye went from job to job—service-station attendant, paper-factory worker, parking-lot attendant. Rene supplemented his income by working as a domestic. The children, who hardly knew what a policeman was, were picked up on their very first day in the city. . . .

For no one was the transition so difficult as it was for Marquette. A thin, intelligent 13-year-old who had all of his life lived as part of a white community, he was suddenly dropped, like a character from a Jules Verne balloon, into a new environment where almost all the faces he saw were colored. In them he could see himself—yet he felt no identity with them. He felt different. He was different. . . .

He was an outsider. He was lost in the impersonality of the 35-pupils-per-class school. Not knowing who he was, or where he belonged—and, even more important where he was heading—his motivation dropped off, he became like a badly tuned engine chugging desperately up a hill. He didn't make it. In his senior year at Fremont High School he became a dropout.

The first time he was picked up by the police was a month before his sixteenth birthday. He was only doing what a lot of the other kids—the ones who always seemed to have change in their pockets—bragged about doing: rifling a coin machine. Telephone booths, coin-operated laundries, soft drink machines—all are easy pickings.

At 77th St. station, the police gave him a talking to. They tried to impress upon him, as they try every year to impress upon a hundred other kids picked up for the first time, what lay ahead of him if he didn't straighten out. It is a brimstone-and-hell admonition, and sometimes it works. . . .

In March of the next year, 1961, he was caught taking wine, cigars, and chewing gum from a grocery store. This time a juvenile court hearing was set, and he went before the judge on May 18. The case was continued, pending the filing of a probation report.

Five days later he and some other kids, including several girls, were hanging around outside a laundromat when an older man began egging them on. Very soon Marquette found himself dared into snatching a purse, containing $18.00, from a woman doing her laundry. The man took the purse, and Marquette was in the process of making his escape, when the police came and collared the girls he had been with. Gallantly he returned and gave himself up. On June 15 he was placed in the custody of the L.A. County Probation Department and sent to a forestry camp.

He stayed there two years, until he was 19 years old. Then he was released on parole. For five months thereafter he worked as a pickup and delivery man for an auto dealer. But he wasn't satisfied. He wanted something better.

"A man may be willing to swallow his pride and eat humble pie if he thinks it's going to get him somewhere," he says. "But what's the use of going hat in hand if it doesn't get you nowhere no way?"

For the next 18 months he worked only desultorily. When he is in his element he has a jaunty, Sammy Davis-like way about him that often charms people and makes them laugh. Emphasizing a point, he will take quick, small dancing steps back and forth, using his hands as if he were sparring, putting his whole body into the conversation. He has a collegiate sophistication, smoking a pipe and wearing fashionable clothes. When he puts on his wrap-around sunglasses, he looks like

a swinger. Within his own age group he is popular. Yet
with the anomalies and inconsistencies of a socio-eco-
nomic structure dominated by whites—a white world
which resembled not at all that in which he had grown
up—he did not know how to cope. It was always a
white man to whom he had to go looking for a job; a
white man who would inspect and interrogate him as
if he were a piece of material for sale. Under those
conditions, he always went on the defensive. He was
made to feel, as he said, "like nothing but a piece of
shit."

Robert Conot, *Rivers of Blood, Years of Darkness* (New
York: Bantam, 1967).

Another racial predicament is described this way.

A new world for the Africans, indeed! The new economic order, essentially urban with its wage labor and
increasing differentiation of work, dominated the social
scene. Europeans were part of the same economic order,
but there was an absence of social relations with them.
Many of the Europeans with whom African miners had
contact on the job appeared to be ignorant of all the
niceties of etiquette, so important to Africans, and gave
them little respect, regardless of their age, sex, or social
position. But there were compensations in this new
world, there was money and the things it would buy;
management was advancing Africans into more responsible and highly paid jobs, and there were opportunities
for individual earners; there was a pension and a savings
system; a union looked after the interests of Africans;
a welfare department provided new leisure activities
such as sports, radio, movies, clubs, classes for adults;
management also gave medical services in a hospital and
clinics. The African Mine Workers' Union and the Mine
Welfare Department, each in its own way, were sources
for some of the compensations and both played important roles in the township.
. . . At the time of my study, gang life, camping

in the bush, and playing in the river had diminished. More boys went to school regularly; but there were not enough schools to accommodate all of them, even if they had all desired to attend. Swimming in the Luan- shya River had been forbidden, because of the danger of catching the disease bilharziasis. In their free time boys went to the Welfare Center, played games, saw movies, and participated in other activities; playing cowboy and boxing were favorite pastimes. Some boys sold chewing gum, sweets, sheets of writing paper and envelopes, old magazines, and the like to get money. Others went to the Welfare Center to pick the pockets of miners who came there on pay-day. The boys thought the Nyakyusa made particularly good victims because they were supposed to be sleepy. The money, whether earned or stolen, was often used to buy tea, bread, and sweets and for gambling with cards. Money, the new goal, is desired by the boys long before they are old enough to have jobs.

There was much talk by some of the older Africans and among Europeans about juvenile delinquency, but I could get little real information about it. I did learn that the term was used broadly and loosely and often for minor misbehavior such as throwing stones, even though no harm was done. Some young boys did engage in petty thievery, usually from Africans. It was my im- pression that juvenile delinquency was limited, partic- ularly when compared to that of any American city. Older Africans tended to think of playing cowbo· and any departure by the boys from traditional custom as a form of delinquency. In fact, many of the boys were going through the modern process of making a break from traditional African authority figures. Politically oriented youths and men were doing the same in their break from European authorities.

Hortense Powdermaker, *Copper Town: Changing Africa* (New York: Harper & Row, 1962).

Finally, here is a description of the plight of a Bra- zilian.

May 22: Today I'm sad. I'm nervous. I don't know if I should start crying or start running until I fall unconscious. At dawn it was raining. I couldn't go out to get any money. I spent the day writing. I cooked the macaroni and I'll warm it up again for the children. I cooked the potatoes and they ate them. I have a few tin cans and a little scrap that I'm going to sell to Senhor Manuel. When Joao came home from school I sent him to sell the scrap. He got 13 cruzeiros. He bought a glass of mineral water: two cruzeiros. I was furious with him. Where had he seen a *favelado* with such high-born tastes?

The children eat a lot of bread. They like soft bread but when they don't have it, they eat hard bread.

Hard is the bread that we eat. Hard is the bed on which we sleep. Hard is the life of the favelado.

Oh, Sao Paulo! A queen that vainly shows her skyscrapers that are her crown of gold. All dressed up in velvet and silk but with cheap stockings underneath—the favela.

The money didn't stretch far enough to buy meat, so I cooked macaroni with a carrot. I didn't have any grease, it was horrible. Vera was the only one who complained yet asked for more.

"Mama, sell me to Dona Julita, because she has delicious food."

I know that there exist Brazilians here inside Sao Paulo who suffer more than I do. In June of '57 I felt rich and passed through the offices of the Social Service. I had carried a lot of scrap iron and got pains in my kidneys. So as not to see my children hungry I asked for help from the famous Social Service. It was here that I saw the tears slipping from the eyes of the poor. How painful it is to see the dramas that are played out there. The coldness in which they treat the poor. The only things they want to know about them is their name and address.

I went to the Governor's Palace. The Palace sent me

to an office at Brigadeiro Luis Antonio Avenue. They in turn sent me to the Social Service at the Santa Casa charity hospital. There I talked with Dona Maria Aparecida, who listened to me, said many things yet said nothing. I decided to go back to the Palace. I talked with Senhor Alcides. He is not Japanese yet is as yellow as rotten butter. I said to Senhor Alcides:

"I came here to ask for help because I'm ill. You sent me to Brigadeiro Luis Antonio Avenue, and I went. There they sent me to the Santa Casa. And I spent all the money I have on transportation."

"Take her!"

They wouldn't let me leave. A soldier put his bayonet at my chest. I looked the soldier in the eyes and saw that he had pity on me. I told him:

"I am poor. That's why I came here."

Dr. Osvaldo de Barros entered, a false philanthropist in Sao Paulo who is masquerading as St. Vincent de Paul. He said:

"Call a squad car!"

The policeman took me back to the favela and warned me that the next time I made a scene at the welfare agency I would be locked up.

Welfare agency! Welfare for whom?

Maria Carolina de Jesus, *Child of the Dark* (New York: NAL, 1964).

These selections, of course, are fragmentary. Any adequate treatment of the topic would require more complete reading from these sources, or the teacher may wish to assign other readings from the great number of paperback sources now available on this subject. Films, too, can help the students gain a clearer perception of the issues involved. For example, "Confronted" (60 minutes) and "The Run from Race" (30 minutes), both available from NET Film Service, provide personal involvement for the student in the problems of integration in schools, jobs, and housing. Another NET film, "The Negro and the American Promise" (60 minutes) offers a wide spectrum of American Negro views, ranging from Dr. Martin Luther King to James Baldwin and Malcolm X.

After the readings and films have been discussed and compared, students might be challenged with this question: To what extent is the experience of black minorities connected with your own experience or that of the white majorities in each society? Even with the obvious racial differences it should be clear that the experiences of migration and urbanization are creating similar patterns of social disorganization and bureaucratization in the majority white society.

A final question might consider whether urbanization is creating less prejudice and more opportunity for black people or whether the reverse is true? This question should be open-ended and offer opportunities for discussion and debate. Brinton's thesis that rebelliousness increases as people's lives improve might be introduced. Factors of living closely together and increased awareness through communication can be discussed as causes of rebellion. The point that people living in rural poverty are less aware of their poverty or see little hope for improvement might also be discussed.

BIBLIOGRAPHY

TITLES DESCRIBED IN THE TEXT

Richard B. Ford, *Tradition and Change in Four Societies** (Holt Social Studies Curriculum, Edwin Fenton, editor, $5.24 hard cover; $1.84 paperback).

Stanley Seaberg, *The Negro in American History* (2 vols., Scholastic Book Services, 1969, $.85 each vol.).

Robert Conot, *Rivers of Blood, Years of Darkness** (Bantam Books, 1967, $.95).

Hortense Powdermaker, *Copper Town: Changing Africa* (Harper Colophon Books, 1962, $2.45).

*Child of the Dark; The Diary of Carolina Maria de Jesus** (Signet, 1962, $.60).

COMPARATIVE STUDIES

A pioneering study of comparative slave systems in the Americas is *Slave and Citizen** (Vintage, 1963, $1.45) by Frank Tannenbaum. *Slavery** (Universal Library, 1959, $1.95) by Stanley Elkins built upon Tannenbaum's study and suggested provocative psychological comparisons between slavery in the United States and prison life in Nazi concentration camps. *The Problem of Slavery in Western Culture** (Cornell University Press, 1966, $10.00) by David Brion Davis traces the roots of slavery in the western tradition from ancient times to the 19th century. Davis offers a comparison of slave systems and

* Titles marked with an asterisk may be ordered from the World Affairs Book Center, a service of the Foreign Policy Association, 345 E. 46th Street, New York, N.Y. 10017.

sharply disagrees with the conclusions of Tannenbaum and Elkins. *Slavery in the New World: A Reader in Comparative History** (Prentice Hall, 1969, $3.95), by Eugene D. Genovese and Laura Foner, offers a wide range of interdisciplinary selections on slavery in the Western Hemisphere.

*Minorities in the New World** (Columbia University Press, 1958, $1.95), by Charles Wagley and Marvin Harris, offers a general comparative analysis of several minorities in the Americas, including Negroes, Indians, Jews, and French Canadians. The Macmillan two-volume American History text, *A Free People* (1970), by Bragdon, Cole, and McCutchen, contains brief comparisons of slavery and emancipation in the United States and Brazil, as well as comparisons with peonage in Mexico and serfdom in Russia.

THE UNITED STATES

Studies of the Negro in American life are now so numerous that one is bound to neglect some excellent studies in being selective. For the larger view of race and culture in the United States, Oscar Handlin's *Race and Nationality in American Life** (Anchor, 1957, $1.25) is recommended. Nathan Glazer and Daniel Moynihan have provided a broad historical and cultural study of the races in the nation's largest city in *Beyond the Melting Pot** (M.I.T. Press, 1963, $1.95). Vivid portraits of race relations in the South may be found in Lillian Smith's *Killers of the Dream** (Anchor, 1963, $1.25) and John Howard Griffin's *Black Like Me** (Signet, 1960, $.60). Northern society may be viewed from the Negro's perspective through a number of autobiographies: Claude Brown's *Manchild in the Promised Land** (Signet, 1965, $.95); Dick Gregory's *Nigger* (Pocket Books Inc., 1965, $.75); John Williams' *This Is My Country Too** (Signet, 1964, $.60); and Horace Cayton's *Long Old Road,* (Trident Press, 1964). A number of Negro novelists, such as Richard Wright, Ralph Ellison, James Baldwin, Chester Himes, Gordon Parks, and James Killian, have supplied vivid and frequently bitter descriptions of America's racial society, North and South. Social analyses may be studied in Kenneth Clark's *Dark Ghetto** (Torch, 1965, $1.75), and the *Report of the National Advisory Commission on Civil Disorder** (Bantam, 1968, $1.25).

BRAZIL

Although the sources on Brazil and South Africa are not as numerous as those dealing with the United States, they are sufficiently rich to provide the American student with materials for comparison. Gilberto Freyre has written a number of books which would be useful. His *The Mansions and the Shanties: The Making of Modern Brazil** (Vintage, 1958, $10.00) and *New World in the Tropics** (Vintage, 1959, $1.65) provide colorful and incisive portraits of historical and contemporary Brazil. A novelist who has drawn upon Freyre's work is Jorge Amado. Amado's classic, *Gabriella, Clove and Cinnamon* (Fawcett, 1962, $5.95) draws a rich, imaginative portrait of Brazil's multi-racial culture.

Freyre's work may be supplemented by the studies of Charles Wagley: *An Introduction to Brazil** (Columbia University Press, 1963, $2.25) offers a sociological view of religion, classes, communities and families; *Amazon Town: A Study of Man in the Tropics** (Knopf, 1964, $2.50) is a fascinating, intensive cultural study of a small Amazon community.

SOUTH AFRICA

The tragedy of South Africa has been pictured vividly in the novels of Alan Paton: *Cry the Beloved Country** (Charles Scribner's Sons, 1950, $1.45); and *Too Late the*

*Phalarope** (Charles Scribner's Sons, 1953, $1.45). A description of the inner hate of black South Africans has been attempted in visceral prose by a white South African in *The Goddam White Man** (Simon & Schuster, 1960, $3.50), by David Lytton.

Black South Africans have also written of their dilemma and many are in jail today for having spoken out against apartheid. Chief Albert Luthuli, author and Nobel Peace Prize winner, has chronicled his efforts on behalf of fellow Africans in *Let My People Go** (McGraw-Hill, 1962). An account of African resistance to the Afrikaner program to reassign native Africans to reservations is given in Gova Mbeki's *The Peasant's Revolt** (Penguin, 1965, $.95). Jorda K. Ngubana gives a history of apartheid and offers a positive alternative in *An African Explains Apartheid* (Praeger, 1963). A more scholarly treatment of the Transkei experiment discussed by Mbeki is contained in *South Africa's Transkei: The Politics of Domestic Colonialism** (Northwestern University Press, 1967, $6.50) by Gwendolen M. Carter, Thomas Karis, and Newell M. Stultz. An analysis from a sociological-historical perspective is Pierre Vandenberghe's *Africa: Social Problems of Change and Conflict** (University of California Press, 1967, $8.00).

FILMS

"Brazil: the Vanishing Negro," Audio Visual Center, Division of University Extension, Indiana University, 30 minutes, contrasts the interracial nature of Brazilian society with the segregated experience of the Negro in America.

South African Essay Part I: "Fruit of Fear," Indiana University, 60 minutes, takes a hard, critical look at racial prejudice and apartheid through films of ghetto life.

South African Essay Part II: "One Nation; Two Nationalisms," Indiana University, 60 minutes, examines political machinery which enforces apartheid through views of white and black spokesmen.

"Lobolo," Contemporary Films, Inc., 267 West 25th Street, New York, N.Y. 10001, 30 minutes, deals with social problems of native Africans and transition from tribal to urban life.

McGraw-Hill Films' *History of the Negro in America Series* (order through Contemporary Films) consists of three films, each 20 minutes in length: (1) "1619–1860: Out of Slavery"; (2) "1861–1877: Civil War and Reconstruction"; (3) "1877–Today: Freedom Movement."

An ABC documentary, "Walk in My Shoes" (Contemporary Films, 54 minutes) presents candid, often searing, statements by American Negroes from all economic strata, rural and urban, famous and unknown, leaving the indelible message that, despite progress, the vast majority of Negroes still feel ostracized from the mainstream of American life. A number of full-length dramas are capable of adding a somewhat different perspective to teaching about race relations. *Intruder in the Dust* and *Raisin in the Sun,* for example (both available from a number of rental agencies), combine fine acting and directing with hard-hitting plots.

SIMULATIONS

A classroom simulation which is stated to be suitable for all grade levels, elementary through Senior High, is "Sunshine," in which students become members of different races in a mythical city and face such problems as segregation. Available from Interact, P.O. Box 262, Lakeside, California 92040.

3

Nationalism

This was the first nation in the history of the world to be founded with a purpose. The great phrases of that purpose are still found in every American heart. . . .

LYNDON JOHNSON, MESSAGE TO CONGRESS

In the face of a compelling need for broader associations, nationalism sets both great and small nations against one another, to their vast peril and at an enormous price in the welfare and happiness of their people.

SENATOR WILLIAM J. FULBRIGHT

THESE TWO QUOTATIONS GIVE SOME INDICATIONS OF THE ambivalent feelings that many people have come to have toward the concept of the nation-state. On the one hand, nationalism acts as a repository for deeply felt loyalties, and it has served a constructive purpose in organizing diverse groups for the purpose of achieving social welfare and economic advancement. On the other hand, we recognize it as a divisive force in world affairs, a major factor that has led to competitive militarism and expansionism in which nation-states have virtually destroyed each other in two international wars during the twentieth century.

No matter what our attitudes, we cannot escape this concept of nation as a central fact in our existence. John Stoessinger describes the dominance of the nation-state in the lives of people in today's world:

> Our world is made up of over one hundred political units called nation-states. There is hardly a place on this planet that is not claimed by a nation-state. Only a century ago the world still abounded with frontiers and lands that remained unpre-empted. But in our time, man can no longer escape from the nation-state system—unless he migrate to the frozen polar zones or to the stars. The nation-state has become ubiquitous. And everywhere it is the highest secular authority. It may decree that a man die; and, with no less effort, it may offer him the protection that enables him to live. When no state wants him—when man is naked in his humanity and nothing but a man—he thereby loses the very first precondition for his fellows even to be able to acknowledge his existence. Whether it be to be born, to live, or to die, he cannot do without official recognition—the recognition of a nation-state.
>
> *The Might of Nations,* Random House, 1969

The basic rationale for placing this aspect of U.S. development into a comparative framework has already been presented. The student will not only gain a better understanding of the growth of the American nation, but will be able to see it as more than an isolated phenomenon—as part of one of the mainstreams of modern history. And again, the American experience can be used to provide a deeper understanding of current domestic and international affairs, and such a comparison of contemporary matters sheds greater light on specific events in U.S. history.

Two ways of providing a comparative framework (and both will be used here) are first to consider the development of the nation-state, and second to view nations in their relationship to each other. The first approach centers around the organizing forces of nationalism, implied in the quote by former President Johnson; the second approach considers the divisive effect of nationalism, which Fulbright has called "the most pervasive of the old myths that blind us to the realities of our time."

In viewing nationalism as an internal development process—as a "form of social organization"—one challenges the traditional interpretation of America's development as unique. Seymour Lipset in *The First New Nation*, for example, uses a series of revealing comparisons with new nations in Asia and Africa to suggest that the new American nation shared problems and challenges common to all developing nations. Lipset's study leads to such generalizations as these:

1. Every new nation must establish its legitimacy, authority, and unity.

2. Charismatic leaders often serve to symbolize the nation's values and aspirations.

3. By organizing a national political party the new leaders mobilize public support for the new regime.

4. New nations tend to be independent and neutral in foreign relations (as was the young United States).

5. The revolution against foreign domination very often provides the national symbols, songs, and heroes.

6. As with the United States, many new nations today

experience destructive civil wars because of the failure to establish consensus on national values and goals.

The second approach stresses nationalism as "a factor of international non-integration." Richard W. Van Alstyne's *The Rising American Empire* (Quadrangle, 1960) explores the developing American nation from this perspective. He "views the United States relative to other national states, possessing like them (and being possessed by) clearly recognizable nationalist urges and drives." This statement is expanded in this excerpt.

. . . The early colonies were no sooner established in the seventeenth century than expansionist impulses began to register in each of them. Imperial patterns took shape, and before the middle of the eighteenth century the concept of an empire that would take in the whole continent was fully formed. . . . In the Revolution the spirit of conquest was a powerful force, and it took about a century thereafter to satisfy the territorial ambitions of the United States. . . . On the North American continent American expansion reached its maximum limits by 1867, the process of advance having been delayed long enough to enable the Canadians to develop the necessary countermoves. The two related drives, south into the Caribbean and westward to China via Cape Horn, continued to the end of the century, when a burst of energy finished off the process in a war against Spain. From the island conquest of that war the United States emerged a satiated power, so that thereafter American statesmen could truthfully say, with Woodrow Wilson, that "never again" would the United States "seek one additional foot of territory by conquest." The sentiment became a fixation, repeated on innumerable occasions, but it is irrelevant.

Richard W. Van Alstyne, *The Rising American Empire* (Chicago: Quadrangle, 1960).

Van Alstyne's approach is placed in an international framework by Carleton H. B. Hayes in *Essays on Nationalism* (Russell & Russell, 1926). Hayes suggests an evolutionary process of nationalism from early nationhood to later expansionism and militarism. He contends that it makes little difference whether a nation-state is democratic or authoritarian. In time, as the young nation industrializes and grows more powerful, its nationalism will become aggressive, intolerant, and self-serving.

Introducing the Unit

To "hook" students on the topic, and to stimulate questions and discussion, teachers might begin by exploring some contemporary examples of attitudes toward nationalism. Have students read the following excerpts from President Nixon's speech about America's role in the world at the Air Force Academy, June 4, 1969, and then contrast it with the poem by folksinger Phil Ochs which follows.

> For each of you, and for your parents and your countrymen, this is a moment of quiet pride. After years of study and training, you have earned the right to be saluted.
>
> But the members of the graduating class of the Air Force Academy are beginning their careers at a difficult moment in military life.
>
> On a fighting front, you are asked to be ready to make unlimited sacrifice in a limited war.
>
> On the home front, you are under attack from those who question the need for a strong national defense, and indeed see a danger in the power of the defenders.
>
> You are entering the military service of your country when the nation's potential adversaries abroad were never stronger and your critics at home were never more numerous.

It is open season on the armed forces. Military programs are ridiculed as needless if not deliberate waste. The military profession is derided in some of the best circles. Patriotism is considered by some to be a backward, unfashionable fetish of the uneducated and unsophisticated. Nationalism is hailed and applauded as a panacea for the ills of every nation—except the United States.

This paradox of military power is a symptom of something far deeper that is stirring in our body politic. It goes beyond the dissent about the war in Vietnam. It goes behind the fear of the "military industrial complex."

The underlying questions are really these:

What is America's role in the world? What are the responsibilities of a great nation toward protecting freedom beyond its shores? Can we ever be left in peace if we do not actively assume the burden of keeping the peace?

When great questions are posed, fundamental differences of opinion come into focus. It serves no purpose to gloss over these differences, or to try to pretend they are mere matters of degree.

One school of thought holds that the road to understanding with the Soviet Union and Communist China lies through a downgrading of our own alliances and what amounts to a unilateral reduction of our arms—as a demonstration of our "good faith."

They believe that we can be conciliatory and accommodating only if we do not have the strength to be otherwise. They believe America will be able to deal with the possibility of peace only when we are unable to cope with the threat of war.

Those who think that way have grown weary of the weight of free world leadership that fell upon us in the wake of World War II, and they argue that we are as much responsible for the tensions in the world as any adversary we face.

They assert that the United States is blocking the road to peace by maintaining its military strength at home and its defense forces abroad. If we would only reduce our forces, they contend, tensions would disappear and the chances for peace brighten.

America's presence on the world scene, they believe, makes peace abroad improbable and peace in our society impossible.

We should never underestimate the appeal of the isolationist school of thought. Their slogans are simplistic and powerful: "Charity begins at home." "Let's first solve our own problems and then we can deal with the problems of the world."

This simple formula touches a responsive chord with many an overburdened taxpayer. It would be easy to buy some popularity by going along with the new isolationists. But it would be disastrous for our nation and the world.

I hold a totally different view of the world, and I come to a different conclusion about the direction America must take.

Imagine what would happen to this world if the American presence were swept from the scene. As every world leader knows, and as even the most outspoken of America's critics will admit, the rest of the world would be living in terror.

If America were to turn its back on the world, a deadening form of peace would settle over this planet —the kind of peace that suffocated freedom in Czechoslovakia.

The danger to us has changed, but it has not vanished. We must revitalize our alliances, not abandon them.

We must rule out unilateral disarmament. In the real world that simply will not work. If we pursue arms control as an end in itself, we will not achieve our end. The adversaries in the world today are not in conflict because they are armed. They are armed because they are in conflict, and have not yet learned peaceful ways to resolve their conflicting national interests.

The aggressors of this world are not going to give the United States a period of grace in which to put our domestic house in order—just as the crises within our society cannot be put on a back burner until we resolve the problem of Vietnam.

Programs solving our domestic problems will be meaningless if we are not around to enjoy them. Nor can we conduct a successful policy of peace abroad if our society is at war with itself at home.

There is no advancement for Americans at home in a retreat from the problems of the world. America has a vital national interest in world stability, and no other nation can uphold that interest for us.

We stand at a crossroad in our history. We shall re-affirm our aspiration to greatness or we shall choose instead to withdraw into ourselves. The choice will affect far more than our foreign policy; it will deter-mine the quality of our lives.

Is There Anybody Here

by Phil Ochs

Is there anybody here
Who'd like to change his clothes into a uniform?
Is there anybody here
Who thinks they're only serving in a raging storm?
Is there anybody here with glory in their eyes,
Loyal to the end, whose duty is to die?

Refrain
I want to see him, I want to wish him luck,
I want to shake his hand, gonna' call his name,
Pin a medal on the man.

Is there anybody here
Who'd like to wrap a flag around an early grave?
Is there anybody here
Who thinks they're standing taller on a battle wave?
Is there anybody here who'd like to do his part,
Soldier to the world, and hero to his heart. . . .

Refrain

Is there anybody here
  So proud of the parade,
Who'd like to give a cheer,
  And show they're not afraid?
I'd like to ask him what he's trying to defend,
I'd like to ask him what he thinks he's going to win.

Is there anybody here
  Who thinks that following the orders takes away the
    blame?
Is there anybody here
  Who wouldn't mind a murder by another name?
Is there anybody here whose pride is on the line,
With the honor of the brave and the courage of the
  blind . . .

Refrain

Another contrast might be drawn between the highly nationalistic short story "The Man Without a Country" and a *New York Times Magazine* article, "Boys Without a Country" (May 21, 1967).

Discussion can center around questions concerning the individual's loyalties and obligations to the nation-state. What issues are raised by such current controversies as draft refusal, income tax evasion, loyalty oaths, and flag salutes? Which would the class consider more patriotic, President Nixon or Phil Ochs? Is it unpatriotic to protest against the demands of the nation-state? The quote by Stoessinger at the beginning of this chapter can be used to raise questions about the nation-state vs. individual rights and identity. Indeed, the observation compels discussion.

Developing Nationalism

Following the introductory discussion, students should be led to search for a definition and meaning of nationalism. How are nation-states formed? Or, how can indi-

"Writing another one of your little protest songs, Mr. Key?"

Marvin Tannenberg, Reprinted from *Best Cartoons of the Year 1968*, Lawrence Lariar, ed.

viduals and groups of diverse religions, geographic environment, values, and loyalties be welded into a single community with an overriding loyalty to the nation-state?

These questions can serve as a conceptual framework for the study of American History through the Civil War period. The initial question—how are nation-states formed?—can be used as an exercise in hypothesis formation, with students suggesting their versions of necessary building blocks for nation-state development. To help them in this process, more specific questions will be needed:

1. What personalities and institutions were influential in establishing national authority?

2. What factors and forces helped to create a feeling of national identity?

3. What forces and personalities were working against nationalism?

The last question will assist students in understanding many of the problems faced by emerging nations in today's world. As Seymour Lipset stated in *The First New Nation:* "Only if we recognize that in the United States the difficulties encountered in making a distinction between the authority to establish government and the authority to govern almost resulted in the failure to create a nation, can we appreciate the tremendous problems faced by contemporary post-revolutionary societies with much more complicated and less advantageous conditions than ours."

In comparing emerging nations of today with the early years of the American republic, the students may find that the contrasts are more striking than the similarities. Bragdon, Cole, and McCutchen (*A Free People,* Macmillan, 1970), for example, in introducing a brief unit on this type of comparative nationalism, do so by stating: "In assessing the difficulties that the United States faced after the American Revolution, modern Nigeria is taken as a contrasting frame of reference." Then, after a brief description of Nigeria's experience as a new nation, the authors point out these contrasts:

> Relative to modern Nigeria, the United States was handicapped by the attitude of other nations. Nigeria has no border disputes with other nations, while the United States was plagued by quarrels with England over the Canadian boundary and with Spain over the boundary of Florida. As we have seen, the English government welcomed Nigerian independence, and it also provided economic aid. Nigeria was a member of the British Commonwealth of Nations and gained valuable trade concessions thereby. The attitude of Great Britain toward the United States, however, was unfriendly, even after the Revolutionary War ended. The English government closed the West Indies to United States ships and deliberately sought in other ways to hamper the economy of the United States.
>
> On the other hand, the Americans enjoyed certain immense advantages over Nigeria in attempting to preserve their union. Although the first loyalty of the average citizen was to his state, and he thought of himself as a Virginian, a New Jerseyman, or a New Yorker, rather than as an American, there was no such legacy of antagonism as plagued Nigeria because of its intertribal rivalries. The Americans were blessed with a common language. Except for a few German-speaking Pennsylvanians and the Indians beyond the frontier, practically everyone spoke English, and nearly all held to some form of Christianity.
>
> The Revolutionary War was costly and destructive, but on balance it helped to promote union. Nigerian independence had come almost as a gift from England, while the Americans had had to struggle for it for eight long years. The war had taught the Americans to engage in a common cause, and it had trained a genera-

tion of able leaders, such as Washington, Jefferson, Hamilton, and John Adams, who thought first of the good of their new country as a whole, rather than of their states.

Bragdon, Cole, McCutchen, *A Free People* (New York: Macmillan, 1969).

The students are asked the question: "Is it fair to make a comparison of present-day Nigeria and the United States in the eighteenth century?" The answer is that such a comparison is valid as long as one remembers that comparison implies recognizing contrasts as well as parallels. Of course, this distinction applies to any comparative studies, but in dealing with developing nationalism it seems particularly appropriate that the point should be stressed.

There are a number of ways to fit the exploration of the students' hypotheses into the standard American History course. The simplest approach would be to assign readings to supplement the basic text. Because virtually no materials have been developed for high school students on comparative nationalism, the teacher is once again forced to piece together readings from available paperback sources. *Readings in World History*, edited by Leftan Stavrianos, provides numerous sources on new national states from a global perspective. Other excellent and fairly brief sources on new nationalism may be taken from *African Nationalism in the Twentieth Century* (Anvil, 1965) by Hans Kohn and Wallace Sekolsky and *Southeast Asia* (Anvil, 1958) by Claude Buss.

Perhaps a more interesting approach from the student's point of view would be to examine the role of charismatic leaders—a study which would touch on practically all the factors involved in creating a nation-state despite the concentration on key personalities. Two books that deal with this aspect of early United States history are *George Washington: Man and Monument* (Mentor, New American Library, 1958) by Marcus Cunliffe and Richard H. Brown's biography of Andrew Jackson, *The Hero and the People* (Macmillan, 1964). If time is limited, half of the class could read one and half the other, or selected chapters could be assigned from each. Both studies get at the crucial question of how each popular hero represented the most forceful nationalist symbols of his day. In each case a dominant political consensus formed around the man, and significantly, both figures emerged during times of crisis for the nation. Washington was vital to national unification and Jackson was a powerful force against threats of nullification and disunion. Both leaders were charismatic personalities who symbolized the values of the new nation to their contemporaries.

For purposes of comparison, assign to individual students biographies (or selected chapters) of recent or new nationalist leaders such as Gandhi, Nehru, Nasser, Touré, Sukarno, Castro, and Mao Tse-Tung. Have each student prepare a comparative critique pairing an American nationalist with a non-Western leader based on the following questions:

1. How did the leaders rise to power?
2. How did they achieve political consensus?
3. What national traits and symbols did they personify?
4. How was unity promoted and how did they confront factors of disunity?
5. What are the major similarities and differences, and how do you account for them?

Following one or two class periods in which students discuss their critiques, their findings can be used to refine and modify the hypotheses they formed on the factors involved in creating a nation-state. On the basis of their study so far, they might find it helpful to construct a chart based on the following format:

	New United States	Nation #2	Nation #3
Type of Pre-Nationalist Society			
Political Basis of the New Nation			
Type of Leadership			
Unifying Factors			
Divisive Factors			

Nation-State (Developed Nationalism)

The second approach to nationalism is from the perspective of developed nation-states emphasizing interactional relationships of nation-state to nation-state. For this approach the proposed *Social Sciences Education Framework for California Schools* offers an excellent conceptual framework suggesting questions, objectives, concepts, and settings for the proposed two-year history sequence of American global history. The study of nation-states comprises the first semester of the second year's course, which is geared to the larger question: How have national groupings and conflicts affected the life of man?

The *Framework* offers a rich variety of settings and situations for comparison. The use of all these settings would, of course, be impossible given the time limitation even within a two-year sequence of courses. For teachers of one-year U.S. History programs the time crimp is even more severe. However, examples can be drawn upon and used in world history and U.S. Government courses in addition to U.S. History.

One way of making use of the *Framework* in a traditional course would be to have the students form a hypothesis based on the question mentioned above: How have national groupings and conflicts affected the life of man? More specific questions as well as discussion guidelines and case studies can be culled from the three *Framework* subtopics which follow:

A) *Framework* subtopic: *Why have societies sought to impose their wills on other societies?*

Concepts

This subtopic inquires into major varieties of aggression and their roots. Relevant concepts include ethnocentrism, racism, religion, secular ideology, imperialism, colonialism, foreign trade and investment. The central question is "What makes groups of people behave aggressively toward other groups of people?"

Settings

Inquiry might begin with the student's own community and the social-psychological processes involved in aggressive behavior among neighborhood peer groups or gangs. Then such cases as the following might be examined: (1) the expansion of Islam; (2) European imperialism and the anticolonial response in Kenya and/or Belgian Congo; (3) United States and its adversaries: ideology and powerblock diplomacy since World War II.

Behavioral Objectives

In studying why societies sought to impose their wills on other societies the student should be able to:

Utilize historical perspective to compare the nature of aggression by small groups or national states.

Classify the causes and results of specific examples of national aggression.

Evaluate the effects of aggression upon the value systems of the aggressors and aggrieved in specific historical cases.

Relate his own values or behavior to value patterns or behavior which have historically encouraged aggression, e.g., ethnocentrism, ideology, imperialism.

B) *Framework* subtopic: *Why do military establishments so universally exist, and how do they affect the societies of which they are a part?*

Concepts

Here students inquire into the reasons military establishments exist, the various forms they take under different circumstances, and the varying roles they play in their societies. Particular attention is paid to the problem of civilian control of the military, and civilian control as opposed to military control of domestic and foreign policy. The question is: "Under what circumstances can civilian control be maintained and under what circumstances will it be endangered?" Relevant concepts include: national security, internal security and police, amateurism versus professionalism in military establishments, and pseudo-Parkinson's Law (a military establishment creates needs which a state must meet).

Settings

The selected settings should exemplify varying socio-political roles of military establishments, for example: (1) Argentina: the military as a conservative socio-political force; (2) Republic of Algeria: the military as agent of radical socio-political change; (3) Prussia: the autocratic state as instrument of the military; (4) Israel: the modern democratic "nation-in-arms"; (5) Japan since MacArthur—an attempt at demilitarization.

Behavioral Objectives

In studying why military establishments universally exist and the way they affect the societies of which they are a part, the student should be able to:

Classify the roles of military establishments in modern history.

Utilize historical perspective to compare the reasons for military ascendancy as specific times in two or more nations' existence.

Identify the characteristics of militarism which have been antithetic to democracy.

Assess the value of a military establishment to the maintenance of sovereignty, and to the maintenance of order.

Assess the nature of relationship between the military establishment and the state in a given historical setting.

C) *Framework* subtopic: *Can man's technological abilities for destruction be offset by his imagination and the desire to maintain the peace?*

Concepts

Students are asked to consider and account for changes in the nature, scope, and destructiveness of Western warfare since the Middle Ages, and then to consider the changing diplomatic methods for controlling war and their adequacy. Relevant concepts include: territorial state, national sovereignty; professional, volunteer, and conscript armies; international law; balance of power; alliance and mutual security; military technology; nuclear deterrence; arms race and nuclear proliferation; arms control; "brushfire" wars; containment; coexistence; "domino" theory.

Settings

The selected settings should exemplify crucial changes in war and diplomacy from early modern times to the present. For example: (1) the 30 Years' War: limited war; feudal levies, mercenaries and conscript armies; the recognition of the sovereignty of territorial states and the beginning of international law; (2) Napoleonic Wars: the "nation in arms"; universal conscription vs. professional armies, balance of power diplomacy and collective peace settlements; (3) World War II: unlimited surrender; the citizen as soldier; United Nations—nationalism vs. internationalization of the peace; (4) the Cold War: containment, "brushfire wars" and the balance of nuclear terror—coexistence or ?.

Behavioral Objectives

In studying the advances in the scope and destructiveness of war in relation to advances in the diplomatic methods for limiting war the student should be able to:

Classify belligerency in terms of purpose and extent of effort.

Classify diplomatic efforts to avoid belligerency as a means of resolving international controversy.

Utilize specific cases in time to compare the effects of war upon the citizenry of belligerent states.

Define concepts relevant to the prevention of the use of military force for resolving national and international problems.

Draw inferences regarding the possibilities of international cooperation in preventing belligerency as a means of resolving international controversy.

BIBLIOGRAPHY

GENERAL

On national development, generally teachers will have to rely upon books of readings and current journals and international periodicals. *Readings in World History,** (Allyn & Bacon, Inc., 1965, $4.96) edited by Leftan Stavrianos, provides numerous sources on new national states but the readings lack a coherent developmental sequence. In *Quest for America 1810–1824* (Anchor, 1964, $1.75) Charles L. Stanford has provided a rich source of documents on American nationalism. An interpretive review of this period is by Ralph Gabriel in *The Course of American Democratic Thought** (The Ronald Press Co., 1956, $6.50, Chapters 7 and 8). As mentioned in the text of this chapter, primary sources on new nationalism can be found in *African Nationalism in the Twentieth Century** (Anvil, 1965, $1.45) by Hans Kohn and Wallace Sekolsky, and *Southeast Asia and the World Today** (Anvil, 1958, $1.45) by Claude Buss.

For the teacher's background reading the following

* Titles marked with an asterisk may be ordered from the World Affairs Book Center, a service of the Foreign Policy Association, 345 E. 46th Street, New York, N.Y. 10017.

books will be most helpful: David Apter's *Political Modernization** (University of Chicago Press, 1965, $2.95) and K. H. Silvert, editor, *Expectant Peoples: Nationalism and Development* (Vintage, 1963, $1.95). Silvert's study includes a theoretical and historical analysis of twelve examples of nationalism. The appendix is especially helpful in outlining a theoretical framework for studying modern nationalism. In addition, Seymour Lipset's *The First New Nation** (Basic Books, Inc., 1963, $7.50, or Anchor, $1.75) is useful either as a text or as outside reading material.

Several source books prepared especially for high school students get at the thorny national-sectional issues by use of the inquiry approach to learning. Three booklets in the *New Dimensions in American History* series by D. C. Heath are especially relevant: *The Ratification of the Constitution and the Bill of Rights*; *The Missouri Compromise: Political Statesmanship or Universe Evasion?* and *States Rights and Indian Removal: The Cherokee Nation and the State of Georgia*. All of the booklets get at the issues of national sovereignty, states rights, and minority status within the developing nation-state. The study, *States Rights and Indian Removal* is particularly interesting and complicated because the Cherokees had formed a separate nation within the state of Georgia. Malcolm W. Langford, Jr., in *The American Civil War: When Does a Nation Divide Against Itself?* (Scholastic Book Services, 1968, $.75), offers a wide range of primary and secondary sources to stimulate inquiry into the causes of the national breakup. Sections on the slavery controversy, political antagonism, and cultural differences raise the question (argued in the secondary sources) of whether the South was not in fact a separate nation.

"Nationalism," University of California Extension, Berkeley, 20 min., black and white, defines nationalism and traces its development in modern times. It presents nationalism as both a progressive and regressive force.

"Rise of Nationalism in Southeast Asia," University of California Extension, 15 min., surveys the conditions that gave rise to nationalism in this area and examines problems confronting new nations in this area.

"One Nation Indivisible," University of California Extension, 60 min., dramatizes how the new American nation survived many crises of nationalism including a civil war that took 600,000 lives.

"Disunia" (available from Interact, P.O. Box 262, Lakeside, California 92040) is a game in which students attempt to cope with problems of emerging nations through divisions on a new planet in the year 2087. To give students a feeling for the interplay between nations during an international crisis, two simulations have proved highly successful: (1) "Dangerous Parallel" developed by the Foreign Policy Association, available from Scott, Foresman and Co., 1900 E. Lake Ave., Glenview, Ill. 60025; (2) "Crisis," available from Project SIMILE, Western Behavioral Sciences Institute, 1150 Silverado, La Jolla, Calif. 92037.

4

Economic Development

Economics has usually been the step-child of the traditional U.S. History course. Normally teachers insert into the course a unit on the colonial economy, with neat little diagrams of the "triangular trade"; a second unit after the Civil War called "The Rise of Industry" or "America's Industrial Growth," which proceeds through Teddy Roosevelt's trust-busting days; and a final frightening welter of initials called the New Deal. In their eagerness to be rid of the topic, teachers tend to ignore the fact that economic development is a dynamic, on-going process, and one that shares an intimate relationship with political and social changes.

The main purpose of a comparative approach to this topic is to enable the student to gain some understanding of the dynamics of the process and to see how it is related to other aspects of U.S. history. At the same time, he will be studying economics in global terms and will learn something of the similarities and differences between U.S. economic development and that of Western Europe, the Communist world, and the developing nations of today.

The format of this sample unit follows the major thesis developed by Irving R. Horowitz in *Three Worlds of Development* (Oxford University Press, 1966): The First World consists of the United States, Western Europe, and parts of Latin America. According to Horowitz, it "is basically that cluster of nations which were 'naturally' transformed from feudalism into some form where private ownership of the instruments and means of production predominated." He considers the United States to be "the most perfect representative of parliamentary democracy and capitalist economies." The Second World of the Soviet Union and its satellites consists of socialist economies with centralized political bureaucracies geared to proletarian values. The Third World is characterized by mixed economies and mass democracies politically grounded in nationalism and socialism.

The comparative studies developed below attempt to give the student some understanding of the principal economic patterns of all three worlds. He should see the problems of the Third World in the light of the developing nations' efforts to gain some sort of "mixture" of the systems developed in the other two worlds, and he will gain some insights into the psychological barriers that separate the three worlds. He should also become aware that, despite some ideological claims to the contrary, neither the First World or the Second offers an example of a "pure" economic system — the United States, for example, contains elements of socialism, just as the Soviet Union exhibits examples of capitalism.

For Greater Depth

For the teacher's background reading or for courses that place a heavy emphasis on economics, a number of interesting approaches to comparative economics have been developed in recent years. Cyril Black in *The Dynamics of Modernization* looks at economic growth as a revolutionary process, beginning with the discoveries of the scientific revolution, which now involves all the societies of the world and which affects all human relationships. Black considers modernization to be the third and most revolutionary of the three "great transformations" in human experience. The first was the emergence of human beings after thousands of years of evolution from primate life; and the second of the "great transformations" was the change from primitive to civilized societies.

Walt Rostow (*Stages of Economic Growth*, Cambridge University Press, 1960), concentrates on the process by which economic growth occurs. He suggests three historic stages in the transition from a traditional economy to a self-sustaining industrial economy.

1. The first stage is establishing the "pre-conditions" for rapid growth. In this initial stage economic institu-

tions are developed which provide cheap and adequate working capital. At the same time, some parts of the economy are growing fast enough that the profits can be re-invested or "ploughed back."

2. In the second and most crucial "take-off" stage, certain conditions are required: a) Productive investment rises from 5% or less of the national income to over 10%. b) One or more manufacturing centers emerge with a high rate of growth. c) The society's institutions become geared to the new economic patterns. Government, for example, smooths the road for continued growth. (Rostow considers the "take-off" period for the United States to have been 1843–1860; for Great Britain, 1783–1802; Japan, 1878–1900; Russia, 1890–1914.)

3. The third stage is characterized by highly productive forces involved in sustained, long-term growth.

Robert Heilbroner's *The Making of Economic Society* (Prentice-Hall, Inc., 1962) includes generalizations drawn from all societies as he traces the rise and development of the market system in Europe and America. His analysis includes a section on development and the forces which have led to planned economies around the world.

Introducing the Unit

The teacher might begin the unit by reading to the class the following statements about the U.S. economy made by a visitor from the Soviet Union:

"The United States has had remarkable economic success, but that does not mean that capitalism is necessarily the best system. Remember, first, that you have been very lucky: wonderful resources, a small population, and no damage from wars. Remember, too, that your industrial revolution had its bad side: the working class was badly exploited, your politicians were corrupted, your cities developed enormous slums, and only the two world wars saved you from the effects of economic depression.

"Now your working class has made great strides. The trade unions have become bourgeois. They have joined the factory owners and the Wall Street brokers to oppress your new exploited class—I mean that lower twenty or twenty-five percent of American society that does not share in the prosperity. Negroes and other racial minorities, the poor white people of your slums and Appalachia. Those are the people who are exploited and it is the exploitation that makes your system work."

Ask the students how they would answer these challenges. To what extent are these statements valid? In what ways are they incorrect or incomplete? What do the students know about economic development in the Soviet Union? What factors have prevented the Soviet Union from achieving a level of prosperity similar to ours?

Following this initial discussion introduce Horowitz's concept of "three worlds of development." Explain that in this unit the students will be examining materials relating to economic development in representative nations of all three of these worlds and will look at them on a comparative basis.

The United States: First World of Development

If no readings are used other than the basic text, the students should read all of the book's chapters on economics at once in order to gain some idea of development. Unfortunately, most texts ignore the period from the founding of the nation to the post-Civil War expansion of industry. Consequently the students are likely to lose sight of the fact that the pre-conditions for economic growth had been achieved by the early 1800's and that in the half-century before the Civil War the United States had, in Rostow's terms, "taken off." In other words, by 1870 the U.S. economy had reached the stage of self-sustained growth.

One simple way to fill this gap would be to use the Stavrianos text, *The Global History of Man,* which gives some indication of the *process* of development. The companion volume of readings contains some good, if brief, source material. The American history two-volume text, *A Free People* (Macmillan, 1970) by Bragdon, Cole, and McCutchen, includes two sections on economic development in the first half of the nineteenth century, using Rostow's stages of economic growth.

If time and budget requirements permit, a successful unit can be developed by using the Scott Foresman high school series, *Economic Forces in American History,* edited by Douglass North. North views U.S. economic growth in a series of stages not unlike those used by Rostow. The following booklets, which are relatively short and quite readable, would give students a good developmental picture of the growth of U.S. economy:

1. *Developing the American Colonies, 1607–1783,* by Robert E. Gallman

2. *Decisions that Faced the New Nation, 1783–1820,* by Douglass C. North

3. *Commerce, Cotton and Westward Expansion, 1820–1860,* by William N. Parker

4. *The Growth of Industrial Enterprise, 1860–1914,* by Lance E. Davis

The students should keep in mind a number of questions as they proceed through these studies; in fact, answers to these questions might even be culled from textbook readings:

1. What physical and human resources did the nation possess?

2. Were there any traditions, such as feudal aristocracy, that hindered economic development? What sorts of traditions, such as equality, encouraged development?

3. What institutions and groups promoted economic development?

4. What role has government played in the nation's economic development?

5. How did economic changes affect society's social values?

The teacher may wish to add other questions to this list or to make the questions more specific. Readings and class discussions should be directed toward finding the answers to these questions. A number of good, brief films are available to supplement the reading. "America Becomes an Industrial Nation" (McGraw-Hill Films, 25 minutes, $25 rental) traces the development of the U.S. economy through the 19th century, discussing the factors which contributed to the rapid transition from a traditional, agrarian economy to a modern industrial one. On the basis of their studies, students should be able to formulate their answers into generalizations such as the following:

1. The United States emerged from the Revolution as a nation with rich, untapped resources and a low ratio of population to land and resources.

2. As a developing country the United States had no

feudal or aristocratic tradition which would prove a hindrance to economic development. Rather early in its history, the United States had developed values of social equality and mobility, parliamentary democracy, and enterprise capitalism.

3. Key influences in the nation's economic development were foreign loans (chiefly British), individual enterprise, and private capital; state subsidies for internal improvements—roads, canals and railroads; federal subsidies for railroads, education, banking; and perhaps most important, federal regulation of land distribution.

4. Government action through local, state, and national institutions provided subsidies, banks, and tariffs but nothing approximating the centralized economic planning of the Soviet Union, China, or even India. The closest approach to comprehensive planning appeared in the Northwest Ordinances, which provided overall direction for the development of new territories.

5. The American values deriving from the Revolution and early nationalism—equality, democracy, material achievement, individual enterprise—became remarkably fixed. Large economic institutions and the consequent need for regulation modified the value of individualism to groups and fostered "team" values. Americans also accepted a larger regulatory role by government. In general American values became more secular and group oriented in the 20th century.

The Soviet Union: The Second World of Economic Development

In studying the Soviet Union as an example of economic development, the class will naturally make contrasts and comparisons with their recent readings on the economy of the United States. To consider some of the more general areas of similarity, you might discuss with the class the implications of these observations by historian Robin Winks:

> Many overseas commentators profess to see striking similarities between the United States and the Soviet Union. Certain similarities do exist. Both nations grew to their present maturity behind a screen of isolation from world affairs, so that both viewed foreign affairs as something of only passing concern. Both nations are geographically large, occupying strategically important land masses. Both nations emerged from a revolution. As a democracy, the United States places emphasis on the common denominator; as a dictatorship, the Soviet Union emphasizes the proletariat, or the common man. Both nations are guided by a sense of mission and have consciously worked to export their principles. Both nations can destroy the world.
>
> C. Vann Woodward, *The Comparative Approach to American History* (New York: Basic Books, 1968).

And the following excerpt from chapter two of Horowitz's book suggests take-off points for discussing some of the experiences unique to the Soviet Union that help to explain some of the contrasts between the economies of the two nations:

> The most obvious fact about the Soviet Union is at the same time the most impressive. In less than a half century, Russia has gone from a backward peasant economy based on rural life-styles to the second largest industrial complex in the world. The present Soviet output of pig-iron, steel, coal, and oil are roughly 80 percent of the United States production figures. But given the relatively slight concentration of consumer goods,

the gap between United States and Soviet productivity is less than the statistics reveal, since this basic production impetus translates itself in heavy machinery, armaments, and other goods which are vital from a perspective of national power. The development of a military machine capable of enormous offensive action, no less than a defensive series of actions, should not be undervalued. As has recently been noted, "as a country considerably less powerful than the USA, the USSR is generally satisfied with less complex apparatus and equipment than the USA and is more inclined to concentrate on relatively few projects, whereas the USA can afford to invest in a great diversity of programmes." All this points to a somewhat less expensive Soviet military and space research and development programme, although the great progress made by the USSR suggests that the difference cannot be enormous. . . .

Like many nations of the Third World, the Soviet Union has been subject to considerable foreign intervention and invasion. And the size of the military establishment represents an extremely important factor in Third World nation evaluations of the Soviet system. At the same time, the Soviet Union has transformed an essentially rural society into a "citified" one. And because of the productive (rather than consumption) pattern, it has done so with a minimum of economic drainage, such as high-priced automotive production, expensive television, and status building. Nor is this urbanization process a simple consequence of a population boom. The Soviet Union has maintained a large but well balanced population (tragically, this is in part the consequence of twenty million casualties in World War Two). Industrialization, military strength, and urbanization are the magic words for the Third World, and represent the achievements of the Second World.

Irving Louis Horowitz, *Three Worlds of Development*, Oxford University Press, 1966.

If the students' basic knowledge of Soviet economic development from previous courses is not sufficient, the pertinent chapter in Stavrianos' *A Global History of Man* should provide adequate background for this unit. The companion book of readings goes beyond the monolithic planning operations of a command economy and covers topics that students can easily relate to their studies of

"Okay, it's agreed. Eight o'clock, to-night, Monopoly at Ivan's house."

Herbert Goldberg, copyright © 1969, Saturday Review, Inc.

the U.S. economy: the impact of the system on the lives of the citizens; the problems faced by planners and consumers; the interplay between the economy and foreign policy.

The following two excerpts, reprinted from an article in the *New York Times Magazine,* indicate in very readable terms the sort of weaknesses and strengths that have become characteristic of the Soviet economy; they also reveal the attempt of the editors to present economic information in terms the average high school student can understand:

> This was a project that would have put to shame the most blatant W.P.A. boondoggle. The road was the Razinskoye Chaussee, a short, five-kilometer link between the town of Balashikha and the railway station of Saltykovka. The authorities had decided to lay a macadam surface over the ancient cobblestones.
>
> The work crew consisted of two men. On their best days they laid perhaps a meter and a half of tar cover; most days they did nothing except bar half the road to traffic. Whether they accomplished nothing or little, however, they invariably consumed an immense amount of good firewood to heat up the tar kettle. The tar was spewed all along the road to melt in the sun or to be stepped upon by passers-by and children. A very large amount of money was spent on a job that would have taken a few days in America. The men on the Razinskoye Chaussee worked for two years and the job was finally abandoned, one-quarter done! . . .
>
> At the Dneiper Dam I met Chief Engineer Kandalov, who bossed the task of reconstructing this severely damaged dam and powerhouse after the war . . . Kandalov was a master of his job and his science. He was interested only in hydroelectric construction. He knew even the smallest details of every important dam

built in the Soviet Union and every important hydro-
electric project built abroad. He had never stopped
studying, and he never stopped working. In his rum-
pled felt hat and cloth overcoat he seemed omni-
present. Like Andreev, he knew his subordinates well
and many of his workers. Now the chief engineer on a
new large dam project, Kandalov will have left monu-
ments to himself in the form of immense dams in many
regions of Russia before he dies.

T. P. Whitney, "The Paradox of Russia's Economy," *The
New York Times Magazine*, February 7, 1954.

A more thorough and satisfactory comparison of Soviet
and U.S. economies can be achieved by using John R.
Coleman's *Comparative Economic Systems* (Holt Social
Studies Curriculum, edited by Edwin Fenton). This inquiry text is designed for a semester course comparing
the two economic systems and contrasting them with a
third, the "traditional" economy, that of the Kwakiutl
tribe of Northwest Indians.

The text consists of a series of 60 readings, primarily
dealing with recent developments but offering a sufficient
discussion of historical trends. By selecting certain readings, the teacher can construct an excellent comparative
study of roughly one week's duration. For example, following a brief reading tracing the historical development
of the Soviet economy from Czarist days, the author presents this introduction to a reading on the modern command economy:

Against the historical background presented in the
previous lesson, we now turn to look at how the Soviet
Union manages its economic affairs today. Two key
points from the historical review have had a particularly profound impact on Soviet development.
First, the Russian people have not known political
freedom in the same sense we have known it. The
builders of Communism did not create tyranny; but

they continued it in altered form from the long czarist past.

Second, Russia began industrializing later than most of the Western powers. Because of this, and because of the mediocrity of much of its cropland, the Soviet Union has continued to struggle with the problem of conquering agricultural inefficiency even though its industrial development has moved ahead rapidly.

The next four lessons examine some of the ways the leaders of the Soviet Union have adapted Marx's ideas and the ideal of the planned economy to meet the realities of economic management and of Soviet life. As you read, keep the following questions in mind:

1. Who makes which economic decisions in the Soviet Union?

2. Why is centralized distribution of key resources a necessary part of a command economy?

3. In the United States, who makes the economic decisions that are made by the Communist Party in the Soviet Union? Who in the United States makes the economic decisions that the Gosplan makes in the Soviet Union?

John R. Coleman, *Comparative Economic Systems* (New York: Holt, Rinehart & Winston, 1968).

A number of readings can be placed side-by-side to illustrate the workings of the two systems and to show how those systems have been modified to meet the challenges of today's world. The following two excerpts, for example, suggest some of the stresses faced by executives in each country:

Instead of being at the top of a hierarchy, he is at the center of a whirlpool of pressures. And those pressures are often in conflict with one another:

The labor unions say: "Give us a wage increase, or we strike."

The board of directors and other stockholders say: "Resist the unions' demands, but don't interrupt production."

The government and such pressure groups as the NAACP say, "Break down all racial discrimination in your hiring."

Some of the vice-presidents and some other pressure groups, such as the White Citizens Council, say: "Don't upset the applecart."

Suppliers say: "Here's a better quality ingredient for your product. Of course it costs a little more."

Consumers say: "Keep your prices down."

The modern executive usually owns some stock in the business, but not nearly enough to control that business. Thus, the executive holds his job not because he owns the company, but because his professional managerial skills serve the company. And, if he is an able executive who can produce profits and goodwill alike, he is a much sought-after man in modern America.

John R. Coleman, *Comparative Economic Systems* (New York: Holt, Rinehart & Winston, 1968).

The Soviet manager is oriented to production. Volume of output is the acid test of his work. Marketing is no problem; finance is a (minor) concern. But the purchasing department is the rock on which the factory organization stands; for supply shortages lead to production shortages . . .

Although the situation is now [1960] in the process of change, raw materials and machinery are still the items of greatest scarcity to the Russian manager. It is these which are his bottlenecks. Labor, of course, is also a problem—but a labor-saving device is not nearly as valuable to him as one which saves materials or which permits more production from a machine. Thus, the Soviet manager tends to emphasize in his daily work different shortages than does the American company president or even the plant superintendent.

Well trained, well disciplined, politically conscious and active, the Red Executive seems a figure permanently established in the seats of the mighty. There is no justification for picturing him as a man in conflict with the Communist Party official, the two uneasily sharing power for the moment. Rather, the industrial manager and the Party secretary are old classmates, neighbors, and colleagues, seeing the world from the same perspective.

John R. Coleman, *Comparative Economic Systems* (New York: Holt, Rinehart & Winston, 1968).

Another interesting parallel study can be made by two short readings on the economic values of the two systems: the first is the Economic Report by President Johnson in 1965, the second is a similar report to the Twenty-third Congress of the Communist Party of the Soviet Union in 1966. A final set of readings makes cautious projections about the directions in which the two economies appear to be heading.

Using the basic questions asked of development in the United States, class discussion can lead to the following generalizations:

1. Russia emerged from the Revolution as a nation with extensive geography and rich resources. The ratio of population to land was relatively low, but the mass of population lacked the skills and education necessary for economic development.

2. The U.S.S.R. emerged from a feudal tradition which stressed social inequality, divine right of Czars, land ownership by the privileged few, and a religious fatalism.

3. Economic development was primarily directed by centralized bureaucracies controlled by the party apparatus. The development of heavy industry was stressed. Agriculture was utilized more for purposes of social control than for economic development.

4. Government plays a dominant if not totalitarian role in directing the nation's economy through a series of five-year plans in which specific quotas and goals are established.

5. Traditional religions and cultural values are undermined by party and state. New values stressing secular-

ism, materialism, and allegiance to the state are incul-
cated.

India and China: Economic Development in the Third World

The basic economic picture of the "third world" is one
of a rather desperate effort to catch up. In a race against
time, the developing nations are pressed by the need to
transform traditional, agrarian economies into modern
industrial states that can successfully compete with the
more highly developed nations of the world. As Horowitz points out: "What binds the Third World together
is not just its being a geographic locale outside the main
power centers, but a psychological unity built around a
social value"—the value being the need for development.

Another major characteristic of Third World economies
is that they tend to embrace neither capitalism nor socialism (although there are exceptions like Communist
China) but are developing economies that represent
what Horowitz calls "a 'mix' rather than a 'pure' system."
Because of the variety of mixtures that is emerging, and
because the nations of the Third World are at such varying stages of development, it is all but impossible to
select any one nation as truly representative of the group.
For this unit, China and India have been selected because of the importance of these two giants as potential
or actual leaders of Third World development.

For this phase of the unit, the teacher will want the
class to gain some idea of the tremendous problems of
modernization faced by Third World nations. A good
way to introduce the topic is to present them with some
readings that will dramatically illustrate the impact of
modern economy on a traditional economy. For example,
a Chinese short story, "Spring Silkworms" by Mao Tun

(this story is available in many high school collections of world literature), reveals the dislocation experienced by Chinese peasants when their centuries-old way of life suddenly becomes influenced by world-wide economic events that they don't even understand. The following excerpt suggests some of the confusion and despair that form the main theme of the story:

Far up the bend in the canal a boat whistle broke the silence. There was a silk filature there too. He could see vaguely the neat lines of stones embedded as reinforcement in the canal bank. A small oil-burning river boat came puffing up pompously from beyond the silk filature, tugging three larger crafts in its wake. Immediately the peaceful water was agitated with waves rolling toward the banks on either side of the canal. A peasant, poling a tiny boat, hastened to shore and clutched a clump of reeds growing in the shallows. The waves tossed him and his little craft up and down like a see-saw. The peaceful green country side was filled with the chugging of the boat engine and the stink of its exhaust.

Hatred burned in Old Tung Pao's eyes. He watched the river boat approach, he watched it sail past and glared after it until it went out of sight. He had always abominated the foreign devil's contraptions. He himself had never met a foreign devil, but his father had given him a description of one Old Master Chen had seen—red eyebrows, green eyes and a stiff-legged walk! Old Master Chen had hated the foreign devils too. "The foreign devils have swindled our money away," he used to say. Old Tung Pao was only eight or nine the last time he saw Old Master Chen. All he remembered about him now were things he had heard from others. But whenever Old Tung Pao thought of that remark— "The foreign devils have swindled our money away." —he could almost picture Old Master Chen, stroking his beard and wagging his head.

How the foreign devils had accomplished this, Old Tung Pao wasn't too clear. He was sure, however, that

Old Master Chen was right. Some things he himself had seen quite plainly. From the time foreign goods— cambric, cloth, oil—appeared in the market town, from the time the foreign river boats increased on the canal, what he produced brought a lower price in the market every day, while what he had to buy became more and more expensive. That was why the property his father left him had shrunk until it finally vanished completely and now he was in debt. It was not without reason that Old Tung Pao hated the foreign devils!

Mao Tun, *Spring Silkworms and Other Stories* (Peking: Foreign Languages Press).

In a more positive vein, students should be aware that modernization also brings about new living patterns and unprecedented prosperity. The Fenton-Ford series offers a number of readings on this aspect of development, as illustrated by the following excerpt of a personalized account by the Indian journalist, Kusum Nair:

In a small village in [Punjab] there lived an ordinary blacksmith named Rattan Singh. Totally illiterate, he used to manufacture locks, small brass ones and some big ones, and also the bit for the horse's rein. Rattan Singh's clients were local landlords who paid him in kind. His house had one brick wall facing the village lane; the others were all of mud. The entrance opened into a yard where he did his work and beyond were a couple of small dark rooms in which the family lived.

Rattan Singh had two sons. He did not send them to school. But neither did he train them to become blacksmiths like himself, though by prevailing standards business was good. Instead he advised the boys, when they were ten and fourteen years old, to go to Batala town, about ten miles away, and learn what must, at the time, have been the latest thing—"saving [sewing] machine repair work." He bought them, almost from scrap, one bicycle costing twelve rupees [about $2.60], which would serve for their transport. This was in 1922. Four years later when the brothers decided to work on their own, their father gave them one rupee and four annas [about twenty-five cents] to get started.

Unable to buy a sewing machine or its parts with the capital at their disposal the two brothers initiated a business on the open pavement of a busy street. While one of them painted simple designs on small pieces of glass which are used for decorating bridal beds, the other purchased a tube of solution and a piece of rubber and offered to repair cycle punctures and earned three annas on the first day.

"The town did not have a single cycle repair shop in those days," they recall. There used to be only an enterprising gardener who repaired punctured tubes in his spare time at the house of the client. "Batala, of course, was more like an overgrown village in those days. In 1926 it had seven bicycles in all."

In 1959, the same town must have at least 70,000 bicycles on the road and the two brothers have become the manufacturers of cycle rims of high quality which find a ready market as far away as Delhi and beyond. Rattan Singh, the village blacksmith, used to sell his locks for a handful of grain. The turnover of his sons' business is in the neighborhood of 250,000 rupees per annum.

The Singh brothers live in Batala now in middle-class style, in double-storied houses which they have built themselves. By caste they continue to be blacksmiths, but not by profession. Their ancestral village is still there . . . not very different from what it used to be in the 1920's. A car cannot enter its lanes, and it has the usual complement of children, goats, cow-dung piles, dirt heaps, mud walls, and a few brick houses. There are green fields of wheat and mustard; sturdy Sikh peasants are working in them. Flights of parakeets catch the winter sun on their wings. Rattan Singh's house is crumbling empty.

Richard B. Ford, *Tradition and Change in Four Societies* (New York: Holt, Rinehart & Winston, 1968).

Additional readings can be selected from the Fenton-Ford study, and for further readings on economic development in China, two excellent and compact studies for high school use are: The AEP booklet *Communist China* (subtitled "Communal Progress and Individual Freedom".) and the Sociological Resources publication *Social Change: The Case of Rural China*. Both studies emphasize the roles of individuals and families in the maelstrom of profound social change.

If the teacher wishes to have the students structure the information they have learned about all four economies, this can be done on the basis of the five questions originally used in considering economic development in the United States. Their answers to the questions can be organized into a comparative chart:

	The U.S.	Soviet Union	India	China
1. What physical and human resources does the nation have?				
2. What kind of tradition characterizes the nation's past?				
3. What institutions and groups promoted economic development?				
4. What role does government play?				
5. How did economic changes affect social values?				

An excellent concluding exercise for this unit can raise the question of comparative values. Reading 59 of Coleman's *Comparative Economic Systems* contains an imaginary interview with an American, a Russian, and an Indian. The following excerpt from that reading suggests some of the issues raised:

MODERATOR: Good evening. *House of Wisdom* is pleased to welcome Mr. C. B. Anderson, an Iowa newspaper editor; Mr. Z. K. Rozanov, an economist in Gosplan; and Miss V. S. Ishwar, a member of the Parliament of India. Our topic this week is, "What Is a Good Society?" Mr. Rozanov, will you begin?

ROZANOV: Certainly. Clearly, the good society must be one that is good for the masses of the people and not just for the favored few. This means that there can be no exploitation of labor by private ownership of capital. Capitalist owners have no interest in using the nation's resources in ways that are best for the nation. They seek only profits. And the good society must put people above profits.

ANDERSON: Now wait a minute—you're assuming that—

ROZANOV: You wait. You'll have your chance. My American friend is stung, evidently because he senses that in spite of its wealth, his own society still has millions of poor people. And its annual rate of growth is so slow as to recall to my mind an old Russian proverb . . .

ANDERSON: I object! Mr. Rozanov isn't describing my country as it really is; he's describing it as the Communist Party tells him to. Let him come and see for himself. He'll see that the average American lives far better than the average Russian. No society has ever produced so much for so many.

ROZANOV: I have seen pictures of your "good society" —with its automobile graveyards and its neon signs and its disgusting rock and rolling dances. You spend much of your resources on wasteful and frivolous junk. You don't produce what the people really need.

ANDERSON: How do you figure that? If you ask me, a good society is a society that gives the individual consumer the freedom to choose what he thinks best for himself. That's the strength of our society. The consumers decide what's going to be produced—they don't leave it up to you and your fellow planners.

ROZANOV: I suggest that you might not want to dismiss planning so cavalierly. A good society needs rapid growth. And we're growing faster through planning than your tired economy is growing without planning.

ANDERSON: Ten years ago, I might have been forced to agree with you, Mr. Rozanov. But we're matching you in the 1960's. So let's wait and see whether your reported long-run growth rate is real and not just a trick with statistics. Let's see whether you keep on growing so fast in the next fifty years. And let's see whether your growth really means anything for the average consumer.

ISHWAR: I've been listening to both of you gentlemen, and I get the impression that you think the good society is the wealthiest and the fastest growing one. Is that all there is to it?

ROZANOV: Of course not. We said that you also have to ask how the wealth is shared—

ANDERSON: And we asked what the growth is used for—is it for the consumers or merely for the state?

ISHWAR: I see. Then I will have to assume that you both think my society is not good. Everybody knows that Indians are poor. And yet, despite our great problems, I think of our society as being a good one—and on the way to becoming still better.

MODERATOR: Well, do you think that India will follow either the Russian or the American paths to improvement?

ISHWAR: The best answer to that question came from our beloved Mahatma Gandhi. He said, "I want the winds of all nations to blow through my house, but I don't want to be swept off my feet by any of them." We want material things, of course. We want an end to starvation and homelessness. And we are learning from the experiences of both the United States and the Soviet Union. But we have our own values. We will insist that the good society has to have more than material wealth.

ROZANOV: Ah, but we agree! We have never said that man lives by bread alone.

ANDERSON: We agree too. We're concerned about the quality of American life. Why we have more symphony orchestras than—

John R. Coleman, *Comparative Economic Systems* (New York: Holt, Rinehart & Winston, 1968).

The students are asked to point out the implied and expressed values of all three speakers, and to show on what issues there is agreement and on what issues there is disagreement. The teacher might carry the exercise a step further by asking the students to supply the contributions of a fourth speaker—a Chinese commissar.

BIBLIOGRAPHY

GENERAL

For a study of the wider impact of the market system upon politics and society in the 19th and 20th centuries, see Karl Polanyi's *The Great Transformation** (Beacon Press, 1957, $1.95). Robert L. Heilbroner's *The Worldly Philosophers** (Simon & Schuster, 1961, $1.75) is a lucid and fascinating study of philosophers who have analyzed various economic systems. In *The Great Ascent** (Harper

* Titles marked with an asterisk may be ordered from the World Affairs Book Center, a service of the Foreign Policy Association, 345 E. 46th Street, New York, N.Y. 10017.

Torchbooks, 1963, $1.25) the same author delineates the challenges of underdevelopment with suggestions for change. Irving L. Horowitz's *Three Worlds of Development** (Oxford University Press, 1966, $2.95) provides not only a carefully reasoned comparative analysis of the United States and the Soviet Union, but offers a cross comparison with the Third World of development. As a general framework for studying economic development W. W. Rostow's *The Stages of Economic Growth** (Cambridge University Press, 1960, $1.65) develops the concept of three stages of development—capital formation, take-off, and sustained growth. *Expectant Peoples** (Vintage, 1967, $1.95) provides an analysis of the response of eight different societies to nationalism and development.

THE UNITED STATES: FIRST WORLD OF DEVELOPMENT

*The Making of Economic Society** (Prentice-Hall, 1962, $3.75) by Robert Heilbroner is an informative account of the development of the American market economy. The final chapters provide comparative analyses of the American and Soviet economic systems. A study of the United States from the perspective of economic development is *Growth and Welfare in the American Past** (Prentice-Hall, Inc., 1966, $3.25) by Douglass C. North. Although North rejects Rostow's stages (or the economic reasons for them) he clearly established his own stages which are not unlike Rostow's. For high school students and teachers (those at least not widely read in economics) a simple and clearly written history of economic development in the United States is the six-booklet series edited by Douglass C. North, *Economic Forces in American History** (Scott, Foresman and Company, 1964,

$6.72). Each book is authored by a noted economic historian and features excellent graphs and illustrations.

THE SOVIET UNION:
THE SECOND WORLD OF DEVELOPMENT

*Soviet Economic Development** (Anvil, 1967, $1.45) by Anatole G. Mazour offers a brief but thorough review of Soviet economic development from its beginnings in war communism through Lenin's New Economic Policy, the various five-year plans and post-Stalin years. The second half of the book consists of first-hand sources: statistical tables, newspaper articles and public speeches by Soviet leaders.

Fictional perspectives on Soviet economic development are offered in *Not By Bread Alone** (E. P. Dutton, 1957, $6.95) by Vladimir Dudinstev, *The New Life: A Day on a Collective Farm* (Grove Press, Inc., 1963, $.75) by Fyodov Abramov, and *Mother Earth and Other Stories* (Anchor, 1968, $1.45) by Boris Pilnyak. In Dudinstev's book an individualistic engineer pits himself against the Soviet bureaucracy, attempting to get his invention accepted. In the books by Abramov and Pilnyak bureaucrats fight losing battles against individualistic peasants who simply refuse to accept or cooperate with modern state-directed policies, whether working a collective farm or conserving forests.

THIRD WORLD DEVELOPMENT

*The Quiet Crisis In India** (Anchor, 1962, $1.45) by J. P. Lewis offers an objective analysis of India's economic challenges and offers concrete suggestions for American assistance. Kusim Nair's *Blossoms in the Dust** (Praeger, 1967, $1.95) offers a series of human portraits reflecting the impact of economic change and development. *Behind Mud Walls 1930–1960** (University of California Press, 1967, $1.95) by William and Charlotte Wiser describes the forces of economic change upon social patterns in a traditional Indian village.

Fictional views of the effects of modernization are found in the novels of Kamala Markandaya, especially *Nectar in a Sieve** (Signet, 1954, $.60), a story of traditional agrarian life threatened by economic changes.

Several first hand accounts of economic change in Communist China are available. Jan Myrdal's *Report From a Chinese Village** (Signet, 1965, $.95) and William Hinton's *Fanshen** (Vintage, 1968), $2.95) are written by authors who lived with and recorded the personal stories of revolutionary reconstruction in China.

Lester R. Brown's article, "The Agricultural Revolution in Asia," *Foreign Affairs*, July 1968, presents an optimistic view of recent gains in the less-developed countries of Asia. A conflicting account of the U.S. role in the modernization of other nations is presented by Robert L. Heilbroner in "Counter-revolutionary America," *Commentary*, April 1967. The author attacks U.S. aid policies for supporting reactionary, status quo regimes. Another pessimistic account (but not an attack on foreign aid policies) is Gunnar Myrdal's *Asian Drama: An Inquiry into the Poverty of Nations*,* 3 volumes (Pantheon, 1968, $10.00).

A highly readable, provocative book arguing for greater cooperation by the "rich" nations in aiding development of "poor" nations is Barbara Ward's *The Lopsided World** (Norton, 1968, $1.25).

5

Interventionism

A COMPARATIVE STUDY UNIT BASED ON THE TOPIC OF INTER-
ventionism is an excellent way to help students gain a
better understanding of international relations in today's
world. Through the use of case studies, they are able to
concentrate on a few specific events; through comparison
of these studies, they can be led to make generalizations
which can then be applied to other events. The usual textbook approach of historical development in one nation too
often leads to the impression that the United States is
the only important actor on the world stage. Instead, they
will gain glimpses of how others have viewed some of our

actions and they will be able to examine those actions
from a global, rather than a strictly nationalistic perspective. The class should gain from their study a less lopsided, less ethnocentric view of American foreign policy.

The study of interventionism can be as current as today's newspaper or tonight's telecast. The main sources
of information, then, might be made up almost exclu-
sively of contemporary materials, and this provides an
opportunity also for teaching evaluation of news accounts.
For this purpose, the book *Interpreting the Newspaper
in the Classroom: Foreign News and World Views* (T. Y.
Crowell, 1970) should prove a valuable teaching tool.
The book emphasizes the gap between image and
reality and the difficulties of getting objective data. At
the same time, it offers concrete suggestions for evaluating
"filtered" information and for using news media in the
classroom.

As an introduction to this unit, the teacher might use
a short classroom exercise developed by FPA involving
the comparative use of newspapers. This classroom unit,
titled *Nationalization of the Suez Canal, 1956: An Exercise Using World Newspapers Comparatively* (Foreign
Policy Association, 1968), can be completed within two
class periods and will give students a better understanding of how national perspectives differ about an international crisis and how sources within the same country
will draw different conclusions about the same event.
This exercise would be particularly appropriate since
nationalization of the Canal was followed by an abortive
act of intervention.

Introducing the Unit

A simple way to start this unit is to lead the class in an introductory discussion of recent or current acts of intervention, such as Czechoslovakia and Vietnam. Help them to draw out information they have already absorbed: Why did the super-power intervene in the affairs of the smaller nation? What were the results of this action? What was the connection between the act of intervention and the larger Cold War issues of East versus West?

In examining a particular case study of interventionism, more specific questions might enable the student to place the event in a larger comparative perspective. Here are some examples of the kinds of questions that could be used:

1. What was (is) the historical and geopolitical relationship of the large nation toward the small nation?

2. What specific events or developments caused the large nation to intervene in the affairs of the small nation? How were these events or developments connected with the historic or geopolitical relationship of the nations?

3. What larger international events—such as Cold War tensions—may have contributed to the intervention?

4. What nations or organizations besides the original contestants were eventually involved in the crisis and why? What roles did they play and why?

5. How was the crisis finally settled? How might it have been settled differently?

Case Studies in Interventionism

If there has been no introductory exercise on the use of newspaper sources, the teacher should warn the class that they will be dealing with material that will present conflicting interpretations of the event they are studying. Where Cold War tensions are involved, they will also have to come to terms with the stereotyped images the two sides have of each other.

Any number of case studies are suitable for this unit, including Czechoslovakia and Vietnam. Two are presented here as examples: the Russian intervention in Hungary in 1956, and the U.S. intervention in the Dominican Republic in 1965. In American History courses, the teacher may wish to add another dimension to the comparative study by adding cases of earlier examples of intervention, such as the U.S. incursions in Latin America earlier in this century.

The Hungarian Intervention

No book of firsthand sources prepared for use in high school classes is yet available. Teachers can, however, select readings from several volumes of primary sources which provide hundreds of autobiographical accounts and news dispatches from various countries. *The Hungarian Revolt* (Charles Scribner's Sons, 1961), edited by Richard Lettis and William E. Morris, and *The Hungarian Revolution* (Praeger, 1957), edited by Melvin J. Lasky, are recommended.

Before assigning readings to the class, the teacher should provide the students with a brief background account and define for them names or terms with which they are likely to be unfamiliar. For this purpose, Tibor Moray's *Thirteen Days That Shook the Kremlin* (Praeger, 1959) is excellent. Readings can then be assigned, either as library or home assignments.

The following brief selections from *The Hungarian Revolt* will give an indication of the differing national perspectives involved. The first selection is an excerpt from a Hungarian rebel appeal broadcast over Radio Free Kossuth:

> Dear listeners, Janos Kadar will now speak to the Hungarian people:
>
> Hungarian workers, peasants and intellectuals. . . . In a glorious uprising our people have shaken off the Rakosi regime. They have achieved freedom for the people and independence for the country, without which there can be no Socialism. We can safely say that . . . those who prepared this uprising were recruited from our ranks, Communist writers, journalists, university students, the youth of the Petofi Club, thousands and thousands of workers and peasants and veteran fighters who were imprisoned on false charges fought in the front lines against Rakosi's despotism and political hooliganism. We are proud that you have stood your ground honestly in the armed uprising. . . . You were loyal to Socialism . . .
>
> We have come to a crossroads in our uprising. The Hungarian democratic parties must (now) choose between stabilizing our achievements or facing an open counter-revolution. . . . We did not fight in order that mines and factories might be snatched from the hands of the working class and the land from the hands of the peasantry. . . . Either the uprising secures the basic achievements of democracy . . . or we sink back into the slavery of the world of the gentry . . . and into the service of foreigners. The grave and alarming danger exists that foreign armed intervention may

allot to our country the tragic fate of Korea. . . . We must eliminate the nests of counter-revolution.

Richard Lettis and William E. Morris, *The Hungarian Revolt* (New York: Charles Scribner's Sons, 1961).

The next selection is from an account by a Soviet tourist in Budapest:

We arrived in Hungary on 19 October with other Soviet tourists. We spent four days touring this beautiful country and were everywhere given a most cordial and hearty welcome. On Tuesday, 23 October, on our way to a theatre we saw crowds of people in the streets of Budapest. They were lined up in ranks and carried placards, many of which bore the inscription "Long Live Hungary!" . . . The students together with members of the intelligentsia and workers were demanding the redress of errors and omission committed by the Hungarian Government. They were legitimate demands.

On that first evening I saw from the hotel in which we were staying a man with a rifle appear in the deserted street. He took up a position in one of the drives and, taking careful aim, began shooting out the street lamps. The lamps went out one by one and darkness enveloped the street. What prompted the marksman to do this? Just hooliganism? Hardly. I think he was one of the bright sparks of the reactionary underground who wanted to create confusion and chaos in the city. Quite soon afterwards there were flashes of gunfire and sounds of battle and we saw wrecked and burning buildings in the streets of Budapest, overturned tram-cars and other vehicles. Firing would die down and then flare up again. Hostile elements were aiming at paralysing the city's life but the workers of Budapest were repelling the rebels. Detachments of armed workers tried to restore order in the streets and prevent looting. In many places, including the area around our hotel, worker's patrols were posted . . .

One member of our hotel staff, a middle-aged man with grey hair, told us: "Our workers cannot have had a hand in this looting and rioting. It is fascism raising its head." And that is what it was. The counter-revolutionary underground was in action in Budapest. Fascist reactionary elements had arrived there from abroad. The hostile venture was gathering momentum and the Hungarian Government asked the USSR Government for aid. In response to this request Soviet military units stationed in Hungary under the Warsaw Treaty entered Budapest to help restore order. The overwhelming majority of Hungarians welcomed this move in the hope that life in the city would quickly return to normal. I myself saw in one street how the people were welcoming the Soviet tanks.

Richard Lettis and William E. Morris, *The Hungarian Revolt* (New York: Charles Scribner's Sons, 1961).

The next excerpt is from an article by an American ("Hungary: The First Six Days" by Leslie R. Bain), which originally appeared in *The Reporter*.[1]

It was 4 A.M. when the first Soviet tanks and armored cars arrived in the city. Overnight another series of events had occurred. Workers in the suburbs had held meetings and drawn up demands generally in line with those of the students. To these had been added several specific points about factory-management councils and general increases in wages. At dawn the workers began marching into the city. Only about fifteen hundred of them were armed. All the rest had nothing but their bare hands and flags. No one was in command. Whoever spoke the loudest or made the most sense was obeyed. Impromptu committees and delegations formed, but the general impression was of huge convergent masses chanting slogans such as "Down

[1] Leslie R. Bain, "The First Six Days," *The Reporter Magazine*, November 15, 1956.

with Gero!" "Punish the murderers!" "We want Nagy!" Later in the morning another cry was taken up that was heard all through the subsequent days: "Out with the Russkies!"

All through this second day furious battles raged. On one side were seventy Soviet tanks, fifty armored cars, and small arms and automatic weapons. On the

Russian tanks in Hungary, 1956

Photo: Black Star Publishing Co.

other were twenty-five thousand students and nearly two hundred thousand workers steadily pouring in from outlying districts. The rebels had at this time about four thousand small arms. To escape the wildly shooting Soviets and AVH men, the insurgents broke into small groups and occupied strategic corner buildings. Some entrenched themselves in military barracks. But still there was no central command, and each rebel unit operated on its own. This lack of organization contributed largely to the heavy casualties. No one plotted this revolt. It just happened.

The second night brought great changes in the situation. Nagy became Prime Minister. The rebel groups disbanded. Only a few remained manning the barricades. The night was quiet.

At this point it did not seem likely that the revolt would continue. It probably would not have gone on but for the tragic events that occurred between ten and eleven the next morning. A peaceful and unarmed demonstration arrived before the Parliament Building to shout for another set of resolutions. There were Russian tanks in the square, but the drivers were smiling and friendly. Seeing a crowd numbering ten thousand arriving, the Hungarian security forces opened fire. The Russians also started shooting. More than a hundred persons died within ten minutes.

Within an hour the people's rage was beyond control, and the rebellion spread.

Richard Lettis and William E. Morris, *The Hungarian Revolt* (New York: Charles Scribner's Sons, 1961).

The final selection is from an eyewitness account by a Yugoslav journalist:

From everyone with whom we talked we have received the reply that there is no danger of abolishing revolutionary achievements, such as returning factories or land to former owners. It is interesting, however, that all people are predicting a right-wing course in Hungary.

Leftist groups are the least noticeable. First of all, the Hungarian Worker's Party seems not to exist. One has the impression Communists are now seeking suitable organisational forms. This will take a long time.

The trade unions were reorganised today. They are abandoning former views, but will ask for Workers Councils.

For the time being the Army is most compact, the best organised progressive force. Although passive for the most part, it was divided in the course of recent events. "Revolutionary Councils" were set up yesterday in the military commands. The commanding officer of the Air Force took the initiative. After being ordered to fire on the masses if they began to march on the headquarters, he refused and "revolutionary committees" were then set up in all services of the Army and even in the Ministry of Defense. Many commanding generals have been dismissed. Today the Army maintained order together with civilians, some wearing badges, some not.

Even today we heard shooting. A real persecution has begun against former officers of the State Security, and today it became a regular frenzy. Groups of armed civilians looked for such officers in various hide-outs. They all defended themselves and were killed on the spot. Crowds gathered around these places and, even more, around mutilated corpses which were displayed in the streets. In front of the building of the municipal Party committee after yesterday's clashes, a former colonel was detected. Found on his corpse was a note showing that he received a salary amounting to 9,000 florins (the average salary is 800 florins). People tore up the money found on him and pinned it to the corpse. Suspects are identified and if they belong to the Security Service they are simply hanged by the crowd.

From time to time Soviet tanks pass through the streets. Obviously they are withdrawing. They arrived as a hanging was taking place, and stopped for a moment, not knowing why the people had gathered. The crowd dispersed, but the tanks proceeded without interfering. . . .

Richard Lettis and William E. Morris, *The Hungarian Revolt* (New York: Charles Scribner's Sons, 1961).

Class discussion should now follow in two stages. First, students should analyze the different points of view they have encountered; second, students should try to find answers to the guideline questions mentioned in the introduction to the case study.

For the first stage of discussion, the teacher should raise questions such as the following:

1. Which of the accounts do you think is most accurate, most objective? Why?

2. What would the attitude of the Russian traveler be toward Janos Kadar? Explain.

3. How would an American correspondent react to Kadar? Why?

4. What particular words or phrases help to indicate the point of view of each author or speaker?

5. Is the Yugoslav journalist sympathetic to the Hungarian rebels, the Hungarian Government, or the Soviets? Or is he trying to be completely objective? Explain your answer.

6. Many Hungarian rebels appealed for U.N. or U.S. intervention. Why was such an appeal made? Why was it not heeded?

In the second stage of discussion, the students will find that their analysis of the different sources will help them find the answers to the introductory questions about the intervention. They should use the same set of questions in their examination of a second case study.

The Dominican Intervention

For introducing students to the Dominican intervention, a brief (13 minute) film, titled *Instrument of Intervention,* is available for sale or rental from Encyclopaedia

Britannica Films, Inc. This film, produced by the National Broadcasting Company, presents a brief background and summary of the crisis, and views U.S. action from the point of view of national goals as well as its international framework. For background reading, a good written account, by an on-the-scene observer, is Tad Szulc's *Dominican Diary* (Dell, 1965).

A good volume of readings for this case study is James Oswald's *The Monroe Doctrine: Does It Survive?* (Scholastic Book Services, 1968), a collection of documents and statements that could also be used to add historical perspective to the subject.

The final section of Oswald's book consists of American versions of the Dominican intervention followed by responses by Latin American newspapers. Although this section is rather short, it does offer a basic groundwork on which the teacher can expand and build. Following are excerpts from a section that juxtaposes the statements of Secretary of State Dean Rusk with those of Latin American journalists, during a news conference on May 26, 1965.

Q. Mr. Secretary, much of the criticism about the American operation in the Dominican Republic would appear to boil down to the assertion that the United States overreacted, particularly with respect to the Communist threat, when the President said on May 2 that the Communists had seized control of the rebellion and that this is making the political way back a bit difficult. Could you address yourself to that assertion?

A. I don't know how one draws the line between overreaction and underreaction and exactly what is right under the circumstances. There is no question at all in our minds that there was a very serious threat for a period, that elements of the extreme left (Communists) had in a very professional and highly organized way seized control of mobs who had been armed, and some of these elements were not under the discipline of any of the recognized political leadership of the Dominican Republic on either side, and that there was a very substantial threat.

And I am not impressed by the remark that there were several dozen known Communist leaders and that therefore this was not a very serious matter. There was a time when Hitler sat in a beer hall in Munich with seven people. And I just don't believe that one underestimates what can be done in chaos, in a situation of violence and chaos, by a few highly organized, highly trained people who know what they are about and know what they want to bring about.

We have had very reliable information from the responsible elements of all groups on both sides about what some of these people were doing, and although it would not be wise for me to go into detail on personalities or individuals, I think that you should assume that at least, whether you agree with us or not, we feel that we were acting on the basis of solid information, and that there were many others working with us down there on both sides in the Dominican Republic, as well as in the foreign diplomatic corps, who thoroughly agreed with our concern about this problem.

Q. Mr. Secretary, M. Peyrefitte (Alain Peyrefitte, then French Minister of Information) this morning called the American presence in Santo Domingo foreign intervention and predicted that this will lead to some kind of escalation. This being an official French government statement, I wondered if you would care to comment.

A. Well, I think that in Paris they might give more attention to the fact that the countries of this hemisphere as a group are dealing with this problem and that this is not a matter on which the French government carries a very active responsibility.

James Oswald, *The Monroe Doctrine: Does It Survive?* (New York: Scholastic Book Services, 1968).

Following are three excerpts from editorials in Latin American newspapers, written during May 1965.

The U.S. government's serious mistake in sending troops to Santo Domingo has had one good effect as far as Peru is concerned. For the first time, at least under our present administration, all shades of opinion from extreme right to extreme left have reached unanimous agreement on one point: they all condemn the intervention of the Marines in the internal politics of any American country (*Expresso,* Lima, Peru).

The invasion of the Dominican Republic by the Marines reduced the OAS treaties, agreements, and principles to so many scraps of paper. In the same way, Germany turned international agreements into scraps of paper when it invaded Belgium in 1914: its government then declared that no scrap of paper would prevent it from protecting its vital interests. Moreover, what happened in the Dominican Republic poses a physical and formal threat to the sovereignty of all the republics of the hemisphere (*Coreio de Manha,* Rio de Janeiro, Brazil).

The Voice of America, official mouthpiece of the U.S. State Department, does not serve the democratic interests of the American countries. . . . It takes absolutely no interest in rightist dictatorships. It approves of any *coup d'etat* favorable to U.S. interests, which means any government that does what the U.S. wants. The Dominican incident offers the latest example of this attitude. The first news about the formation of the civilian-military junta came from the Voice of America, which terms the man whom the Dominican people chose to be their constitutional president a "rebel colonel" while calling Mr. Imbert Barreras "president" of the civilian-military junta. The OAS, the U.S. ambassador, and the Voice of America broadcasts have good sources of accurate information on the invasion and its consequences. But to make use of these sources does not seem to conform with the interests of the United States (*La Nacion,* Santo Domingo).

James Oswald, *The Monroe Doctrine: Does It Survive?* (New York: Scholastic Book Services, 1968).

In this study we have used intervention in an overt military sense. There are numerous examples of less heavyhanded interventionism which might be explored by the class—training anti-guerrilla forces, CIA advisory groups, diplomatic influence, etc. Most likely some type of interventionism will be in process at the time the unit is being studied.

A concluding evaluation might explore the larger implications of interventionism. For example: Will international relations continue to be dominated by super powers? Do super powers actually dominate world affairs, or do they simply respond to crises initiated by small nations? Could the problems or crises leading to interventionism have been handled by the United Nations or regional organizations? Why or why not?

BIBLIOGRAPHY

GENERAL

Titles described in the text:

Interpreting the Newspaper in the Classroom: Foreign News and World Views (T. Y. Crowell, 1970).

*Nationalization of the Suez Canal, 1956: An Exercise Using World Newspapers Comparatively** (Foreign Policy Association, 1968, 1969, $2.50 for classroom kit and teacher's guide).

The comprehensive study of nation-states and international politics by John Stoessinger, *The Might of Nations** (Random House, 1961, $6.95), incorporates several case studies of intervention. The value of Stoessinger's study is in providing a larger framework of international relations. Richard Barnet's *Intervention and Revolution** (World, 1968, $6.95) considers five cases of U.S. postwar intervention and places these experiences within the context of Cold War competition and confrontation with Third World revolutions. Ronald Steel's *Pax Americana** (Viking, 1967, $1.85), less critical than Barnet's study, analyzes the causes of America's postwar intervention.

For a refreshingly different look at interventionism, as well as other aspects of international affairs, see Roger Fisher's *International Conflict For Beginners* (Harper & Row, 1969, $5.95).

* Titles marked with an asterisk may be ordered from the World Affairs Book Center, a service of the Foreign Policy Association, 345 E. 46th Street, New York, N.Y. 10017.

THE HUNGARIAN INTERVENTION

Titles described in the text:

*The Hungarian Revolt,** edited by Richard Lettis and William E. Morris (Charles Scribner's Sons, 1961, $2.75).

*The Hungarian Revolution,** edited by Melvin J. Lasky (Praeger, 1957). Tibor Moray, *Thirteen Days That Shook the Kremlin* (Praeger, 1959).

Another source of eyewitness accounts, presented in highly readable form, is *The Bridge at Andau* (Bantam, 1967, $.50). Historical perspective is provided in *Ten Years After** (Holt, Rinehart & Winston, 1966, $5.95).

THE DOMINICAN INTERVENTION

Titles described in the text:

James Oswald, *The Monroe Doctrine: Does It Survive?* (Scholastic Book Services, 1968, $.75).

Tad Szulc, *Dominican Diary* (Dell, 1965, $.75).

The sense of immediacy gained by reading Szulc's account may be reinforced by a more scholarly analysis provided by the Ninth Hammarskjold Forum, *The Dominican Republic Crisis, 1965** (Oceana Publications, 1967, $2.45). A careful review of the chronology of events is combined with coverage of the Inter-American Commission on Human Rights.

OTHER INTERVENTIONS

A number of excellent and brief studies are available on the British-French-Israeli intervention in the Suez crisis of 1956. *No End of a Lesson** (Potter, 1967, $5.00) by Anthony Nutting is an interesting personal memoir by a British official who sacrificed his career by resigning in protest over the Suez affair. *Suez** (Harper & Row, 1967, $5.95) by Hugh Thomas is more objective and less critical of British actions. Thomas agrees with Nutting, however, that the operation was doomed from the start as surely as British imperialism itself was doomed. One of the most valuable studies is the written version of the British Broadcasting Company series published as *Suez: Ten Years After** (Random House, 1966, $1.95) by Peter Calvocoressi. Many of the principal participants were interviewed giving the book a sense of immediacy as well as history.

Regarding other recent excursions by the U.S. into the Caribbean, the disastrous Bay of Pigs invasion is chronicled in two journalistic accounts: *The Cuban Invasion* (Ballantine, 1962, $3.95) by Tad Szulc; and *The Bay of Pigs* (Dell, 1964, $7.95) by Haynes Johnson. Among several books on the Cuban Blockade, Elie Abel's *The Missile Crisis** (J. B. Lippincott Company, 1966, $5.95) and *Collision Course* (Praeger, 1963, $2.25) by Henry M. Pachter are thoroughly detailed studies as suspenseful as fiction.

Of course there has been a multitude of material written about the U.S. involvement in Vietnam. For high school use, an excellent study unit has been prepared by the Boston Area Teaching Project (*Vietnam Curriculum*-New York Review of Books, 1968, $10.00 per set) which presents a wide collection of documents, government position papers and newspaper accounts reflecting the full spectrum of opinion regarding the crisis and the history leading up to it. Number 188 of the FPA *Headline Series, Vietnam: Issues for Decision** (Foreign Policy Association, 1968, $.85) is an objective presentation of the decision options available to the United States.

A journalistic account of the Soviet intervention in Czechoslovakia is *Prague's 200 Days: The Struggle for Democracy in Czechoslovakia** (Praeger, 1969, $5.95)

by H. Schwartz. *Eastern Europe After Czechoslovakia**
(Number 195 of the FPA *Headline Series*, 1969, $.85)
by Alexander J. Groth, discusses the impact of the crisis
on the Communist bloc nations.

FILMS

"Great Powers in Action" Audio Visual Center, Division
of University Extension, Indiana University, 30 min.,
black and white, examines pros and cons of armed intervention by major powers in disputes of other nations.

"Revolt in Hungary," Association Industry Films, 135
Peter Street, Toronto 2B, 28 min., black and white, offers
a firsthand look at the 1956 Hungarian uprising and
Soviet intervention.

"Crisis at Suez," Association Films, 28 min., black and
white, describes with original newsreel footage the ill-
fated Israeli invasion of the Sinai Peninsula and the
British-French intervention in Egypt.

"Cuba—Bay of Pigs," University of Southern California,
Film Distribution Center, University Park, Los Angeles,
California 90007, examines the background and state of
affairs which led to Cuban invasion and reason for its
failure.

"Revolt in Hungary," CBS News "20th Century" Production, 27 mins. McGraw-Hill Films, "Made from footage taken by a member of the Hungarian underground
and smuggled out of the country, the film documents
the events leading up to the rebellion and reveals the
savagery of the Russian Army in crushing the revolt."

CURRICULUM PROJECTS

Course material under the title "Decision Making in
the International System," developed by the Lincoln

Filene Center Program in Research and Development in the Social Studies (Dr. John S. Gibson, director, Lincoln Filene Center, Tufts University, Medford, Mass. 02155) includes units on the Hungarian, Dominican, and Suez interventions.

6

Additional
Comparative Studies

THE FIVE MAJOR TEACHING UNITS PRESENTED IN THIS BOOK have been described in some detail so that teachers can make use of them with as little additional preparation as possible. These five units, of course, do not exhaust the possibilities for comparisons. Following are several subjects that can be developed with a minimum of preparation and reading.

Frontier Movements

The migration of Europeans into the "open spaces" of the world was a phenomenon which exhibited common elements in many areas: exploration and colonization, migration and settlement, conflict with native peoples, exploitation of resources, economic development, the growth of urban centers and transportation networks. In nearly all of the transplanted European settlements, nationalist independence movements eventually developed. In many ways the American experience was unique; in other ways it was remarkably similar to frontier movements in Australia, Siberia, Latin America, Canada, and South Africa. A study of both the parallels and the contrasts will help the student to gain a fuller understanding of this phase of our history.

The unit could be organized around questions such as these:

1. In light of the frontier movements studied, what impact did these experiences exert on institutions and national character?

2. In what ways was the American Frontier experience similar to that of other societies? In what ways was it different?

3. What generalizations can be made about frontier societies compared to urban societies?

Several possibilities for frontier comparisons, including the Russian and Chinese, are explored in *The Frontier in Perspective* (The University of Wisconsin Press, 1967, $2.25) edited by Walker D. Wyman and Clifton B. Kroeber. Essays by Seymour Lipset and Ray Allen Billington in Woodward's *Comparative Approach to American History* * (Basic Books, Inc., 1968) suggest the possibilities as well as the limitations of comparative frontier

* This book may be ordered from the World Affairs Book Center, a service of the Foreign Policy Association, 345 E. 46th Street, New York, N.Y. 10017.

history. *The Western Frontier* (Harper & Row, 1956) by Billington summarizes most of the arguments for and against the Turner frontier thesis.

As a specific area of comparison, an interesting sub-unit could be built around an analysis of the American and Australian frontier movements. In *Bush and Backwoods* (Michigan State University Press, 1959, $3.50), H. C. Allen finds close parallels between the two experiences. From the perspective of literature and myth, comparisons can be made between Russell Ward's *The Australian Legend* (Oxford University Press, 1958, $6.50) and Henry Nash Smith's *Virgin Land* (Vintage, 1950, $1.45). The fiction and other writings of Joseph Murphy could be studied in conjunction with American writers such as Mark Twain and Walt Whitman. In a similar vein, Nevil Shute's *Beyond the Black Stump* (Morrow, 1956, $.60) a warmly human story of an Australian outland girl who came to live with an American family in Oregon, is a rich source of comparative frontier values.

In a recent essay titled "The Unamerican Nature of Canadian History" (*The Westerners*, 1968), Robin Winks has suggested that from a frontier perspective Canadian history differs from the United States in three critical respects: Unlike the United States the Canadian frontier did *not* provide a "highly varied set of environments in which complementary agriculture and industry might advance"; Canada did *not* enjoy the "free security" offered by the American frontier; nor did local conditions provide the reasons and means for local law; for in Canada, "the laws preceded the settlement."

In spite of differences, Canadian-American history offers several frontier comparative studies which might serve to enlighten students in the United States about the development of an often neglected neighbor: a comparison of the feudal seigneur with the feudal cavalier of the American South and comparisons of Indian policy, land policy, railroad development, and pioneer farming. *A Free People* (2 vols., Macmillan, 1970) by Bragdon, Cole, and McCutchen, contains numerous comparisons between United States and Canadian history, including frontier movements.

The following scholarly analyses would be helpful for the teacher's preparation: Paul Sharp, "Some Comparative Studies of Canadian, American and Australian Settlement," *The Pacific Historical Review* (November, 1955); and Dietrich Gerhard's "The Frontier in Comparative View," *Comparative Studies in Society and History* (March, 1959).

Rather than have the entire class examine case studies of one or two other frontier movements, the teacher might wish to have individuals prepare reports on a number of different areas. Some examples and sources for information are:

1. Siberia—Donald Treadgold, *The Great Siberian Migration* (Princeton University Press, 1957, $6.00)
2. Argentina—James R. Scobie, *Argentina* (Oxford University Press, 1957, $6.00)
3. Brazil—Charles Wagley, *An Introduction to Brazil* (Columbia University Press, 1963, $2.25)

Poverty

As Oscar Lewis has observed, poverty exhibits a universal quality, whatever culture it happens to be a part of; the conditions of poverty are so powerful that there is a "culture" of poverty. Considering the proportions of this world-wide tragedy, it is hard to think of a subject that could make a U.S. studies course more vitally relevant to today's world.

A study unit on this subject might deal with the following questions:

1. Does poverty have similar manifestations in different societies?

2. Some people say that poverty in the United States is "hidden." To what extent is this correct?

3. What are some of the reasons for poverty in the United States as compared to its existence in other areas of the world?

4. What is the relationship of urbanization, population growth, and race relations to poverty?

5. How can poverty be eliminated?

Because interpretations of American culture have for so long stressed wealth as a key to understanding national character, some critics have questioned whether America has the capacity to empathize with the poverty-stricken Third World. Historian David Potter views Americans throughout their history as *People of Plenty* (University of Chicago Press, 1954, $1.50) and John K. Galbraith suggests the best description for present-day America in *The Affluent Society** (Mentor, 1958, $.75).

Nevertheless, as Galbraith suggested in his provocative study, a substantial segment of America is living in poverty. The rising wealth of the middle class has tended to obscure this serious deprivation. In the 1960's, poverty was finally made visible by a series of books and articles, by protests of the urban poor, and by a national anti-

---

* Titles marked with an asterisk may be ordered from the World Affairs Book Center, a service of the Foreign Policy Association, 345 E. 46th Street, New York, N.Y. 10017.

poverty program. Michael Harrington's *The Other America** (Penguin, 1962, $.95) drew a particularly revealing portrait of poverty in America. Ben H. Bagdikian's articles and books, *In the Midst of Plenty** (Signet, 1965, $.75) gave further evidence of the seriousness of poverty in America.

In addition to the above books a study of the culture of poverty in America by high school students might include such books as Claude Brown's *Manchild in the Promised Land** (Signet, 1965, $.95), a gut-level account of a black youngster growing up in Harlem; *La Vida,** by Oscar Lewis (Random House, 1966, $7.00), which describes the life of Puerto Rican families in the United States and Puerto Rico. The recent *Report of the National Advisory Commission on Civil Disorders** (Bantam, 1968, $1.25) chronicles in unmistakable terms the combined efforts of poverty and racism in creating violence. Practically any current film catalogue will suggest a number of films documenting this national crisis and the sporadic efforts to correct it.

For comparative perspective, the excellent studies by Oscar Lewis provide exciting and relevant first-hand accounts of poverty. *Five Families** (Mentor, 1959, $.95) and *The Children of Sanchez** (Vintage, 1961, $2.95) are especially revealing accounts of poverty in Mexico. Two other highly readable studies afford additional comparative perspective on poverty in Latin America: *Child of the Dark** by Maria de Jesus (NAL, 1964, $.75) is a desperate and gripping diary account by a woman of the Sao Paulo, Brazil, *favela*. In *The Barrios of Manta** (Signet, 1965, $.75) an American Peace Corps couple, Rhoda and Earle Brooks, tell of their experience in a small Ecuadorian fishing village.

While it is impossible to list studies and dramatic accounts of poverty in all areas of the world, a number of general accounts of poverty can be mentioned as take-off points for further reading and study. The following are particularly recommended: Arthur Blaustein and Roger R. Woock, editors, *Man Against Poverty: World War III** (Vintage, 1968, $2.45); Franz Fanon, *The Wretched of the Earth** (Grove Press, 1965, $1.95); Robert Heilbroner, *The Great Ascent** (Harper & Row, 1963, $1.25); Barbara Ward, *The Rich Nations and the Poor Nations* (W. W. Norton, 1962, $1.25).

Imperialism

A contemporary historian has suggested that "One suspects that the American imperial experience is comparable to that of other nations only briefly, somewhat incidentally, and then but half the time." This "incidental" imperialism did, however, involve substantial extension into Asia and Latin America at the same time that European nations and Japan were establishing colonial beach-heads in the Pacific and carving out spheres of influence in Asia and Africa.

Several approaches to a comparative study of imperialism are possible. An excellent comparative study could be pursued centering on China in the early years of the twentieth century, using the imperial incursions of various European countries, Russia, Japan, and the United States. Another approach might be to undertake a comparative parallel study with Japan, a country that engaged the United States in a series of international involvements for over half a century.

Studying the imperial rivalry of Japan and the United States for an extended period would provide a richer historical background for the furious conflict that erupted at Pearl Harbor. It was ironically the United States that, with the threat of Admiral Perry's naval cannons, forcibly opened Japan's tightly closed harbors to international trade. From that historic date in 1857, the histories of Japan and the United States meet and intertwine at many points. Both nations developed industrially at relatively the same time. Both nations built powerful navies and trounced traditional world powers during the same era— the United States defeating Spain in 1898 and Japan smashing both China and Russia in 1894–1895 and 1904, respectively. Both countries, new on the world scene, developed imperial interests and commitments in the Pacific and viewed each other as rivals.

A unit based on the expansionist impulses of the United States and Japan could deal with the following questions:

1. What are some of the causes of imperialist expansion?

2. What rationalizations are used to explain imperialist adventures?

3. What is the connection between imperialism and war?

An excellent study for this approach is Akirn Iziye's *Across the Pacific** (Harcourt, Brace and World, 1967, $8.50). Selected readings could also be assigned from Edwin Reischauer's *The United States and Japan** (The Viking Press, 1960, $1.85). From the Japanese perspective, R. Storry's *A Short History of Modern Japan** (Penguin, 1960, $1.25) offers coverage of domestic events which pushed Japan toward imperialism. For more thorough analysis of U.S. involvement assign appropriate sections from *Expansionists of 1898* (Quadrangle Books, 1964,

$2.45) by Julius W. Pratt and George Kennan's *American Diplomacy 1900–1950** (Mentor, 1951, $.75). An NET film, "The United States and Japan" (30 min.) presents a brief review of relations between the two countries from the days of Commodore Perry to the present.

For a larger view of imperialism, or for the teacher's background reading, *The Colonial Empires: A Comparative Survey from the Eighteenth Century* (Dell, 1967, $8.00) is suggested. Fieldhouse devotes little space to the American empire, but his coverage of international imperialism does provide an appropriate framework for comparing the United States imperial venture with those of other countries.

Two Roads Toward Progress: The United States and Mexico

Throughout the course in United States history, American students confront the history of Mexico—in studies of the Monroe Doctrine, Texas independence, California, the Mexican War, interventionism under Woodrow Wilson, the Good Neighbor era, and, more recently, the Alliance for Progress. In most instances, the Mexican viewpoint receives little if any attention. The historical interaction is viewed solely from the American perspective.

Several of the confrontations between Mexico and the United States suggest excellent opportunities for comparison. The use of Mexican sources for the Mexican War era, for example, would provide a broader canvass and redress the limited perspective that most students obtain of that significant era.

During the twentieth century, the histories of the

United States and Mexico were interwoven at many points. In the early part of the century the United States occupied Vera Cruz and invaded Mexican territory in a vain attempt to capture the revolutionary leader, Pancho Villa. American-owned property in Mexico was nationalized during the 1930's under Cardenas and relations were extremely tense. Friendly ties were strengthened when Franklin Roosevelt chose to follow a conciliatory, cooperative approach to Mexican-American relations.

A major parallel between the two countries is that each developed a progressive ethic and program during the twentieth century. The Mexican ideal of progress was constructed on the ideals of the Revolution, and carried a proletarian thrust stressing "Indianismo," the celebration of Indian cultural values. The progressive ideal in the United States developed under Theodore Roosevelt and Woodrow Wilson and reached its fullest expression in the administration of Franklin Roosevelt. At approximately the same time the Mexican revolutionary program achieved its most far-reaching reforms under Lazaro Cardenas. Since the 1930's the political and social histories of both countries have been concerned with consolidating and institutionalizing the reforms of Cardenas and Roosevelt.

Another value of studying the Mexican example stems from its closeness to the underdeveloped "third world." Learning about a developing country so close to home should give American students a greater appreciation of the problems (and the successes) experienced by the great majority of countries in the world.

Questions around which to organize the study might include these:

1. What are the similarities and differences between

the ideas of progress which have developed in each country?

2. Is modernization creating similar problems in both countries?

3. Which country do you feel has been more progressive and why?

4. Which model would you use if you were the leader of an underdeveloped country?

The sources for progressive history in the United States, even for high school students, are numerous. Ganley's *The Progressive Movement* (Macmillan, 1964, $1.32), Dexter Perkins' *The New Age of Franklin Roosevelt** (University of Chicago Press, 1957, $1.95) and Edward H. Merrill's *Responses to Economic Collapse: The Great Depression of the 1930's* (D. C. Heath, 1964, $1.40) provide excellent reading for secondary students.

A detailed study of the long-range effects of the Mexican Revolution, edited by Stanley Ross, is *Is the Mexican Revolution Dead?** (Knopf, 1966, $2.50). In this volume a number of Mexican historians and writers offer conflicting views on the Mexican experience since the Revolution. Other sources include Frank Tannenbaum's *Mexico: The Struggle for Peace and Bread** (Knopf, 1950, $4.95) and the latter portion of *Many Mexicos** (University of California, 1966, $1.95) by Lesley Byrd Simpson. For a contemporary essay stressing the positive aspects of Mexican-American relations, an article in the *Reporter* (April 18, 1968), "Mexico: The Problem of Proximity," by Gladys Delmas provides a brief, concise survey.

A similar unit can be constructed around comparisons between the United States and Canada. There are some

---

* Titles marked with an asterisk may be ordered from the World Affairs Book Center, a service of the Foreign Policy Association, 345 E. 46th Street, New York, N.Y. 10017.

useful titles for such a unit: A. B. Hodgetts, *Decisive Decades*—Canadian history in the twentieth century (Thomas Nelson & Sons, 1960); Edgar McInnis, *Canada: A Political and Social History** (Holt, Rinehart & Winston, 1967, $10.50); Gerald S. Graham, *A Concise History of Canada* (Viking, 1968); John A. MacDonald, Vol. I "The Young Politician," and Donald Creighton, Vol. II "The Old Chieftain" (Macmillan of Canada, 1966); Gerald M. Craig, *The United States and Canada** (Harvard University Press, 1968, $7.95); Cameron Nish (ed.) *Canadian Historical Documents* series: Vol. I "The French Regime," D. B. Waite (ed.), Vol. II "Pre-Confederation," Vol. III, R. C. Brown and M. E. Prang (eds.), "Confederation to 1949," (Prentice-Hall of Canada, 1965 and 1966, $2.95 ea.).